T0191383

# POCKET STUDY SKILLS

*Series Editor:* **Kate Williams**,
*Oxford Brookes University, UK*
Illustrations by Sallie Godwin

For the time-pushed student, the *Pocket Study Skills* pack a lot of advice into a little book. Each guide focuses on a single crucial aspect of study giving you step-by-step guidance, handy tips and clear advice on how to approach the important areas which will continually be at the core of your studies.

**Published**

14 Days to Exam Success
Analyzing a Case Study
Brilliant Writing Tips for Students
Completing Your PhD
Doing Research (2nd edn)
Getting Critical (2nd edn)
Planning Your Dissertation
Planning Your Essay (2nd edn)
Planning Your PhD
Posters and Presentations
Reading and Making Notes (2nd edn)

Referencing and Understanding Plagiarism
(2nd edn)
Reflective Writing
Report Writing
Science Study Skills
Studying with Dyslexia (2nd edn)
Success in Groupwork
Time Management
Where's Your Argument?
Writing for University (2nd edn)

# POCKET STUDY SKILLS
## Janet Godwin

# STUDYING WITH DYSLEXIA
## SECOND EDITION

 macmillan international HIGHER EDUCATION

 RED GLOBE PRESS

© Janet Godwin 2018

All rights reserved. No reproduction, copy or transmission of this
publication may be made without written permission.

No portion of this publication may be reproduced, copied or transmitted
save with written permission or in accordance with the provisions of the
Copyright, Designs and Patents Act 1988, or under the terms of any licence
permitting limited copying issued by the Copyright Licensing Agency,
Saffron House, 6–10 Kirby Street, London EC1N 8TS.

Any person who does any unauthorized act in relation to this publication
may be liable to criminal prosecution and civil claims for damages.

The author has asserted her right to be identified as the author of this
work in accordance with the Copyright, Designs and Patents Act 1988.

First edition 2012
Second edition published 2018 by
PALGRAVE

Red Globe Press in the UK is an imprint of Springer Nature Limited,
registered in England, company number 785998, of 4 Crinan Street,
London, N1 9XW.

Red Globe Press® is a registered trademark in the United States, the
United Kingdom, Europe and other countries.

ISBN 978–1–352–00039–9 paperback

This book is printed on paper suitable for recycling and made from fully
managed and sustained forest sources. Logging, pulping and manufacturing
processes are expected to conform to the environmental regulations of the
country of origin.

A catalogue record for this book is available from the British Library.

A catalog record for this book is available from the Library of Congress.

# Contents

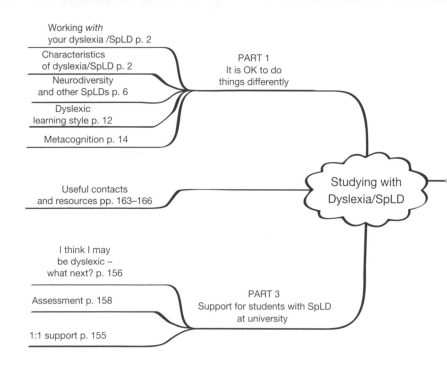

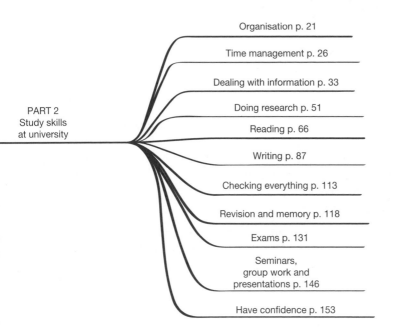

Contents

# Acknowledgements

My thanks go to my students, who have taught me everything I know about how to support them. I never cease to be inspired by both their determination and the effort made to achieve academically, despite their SpLD (specific learning difference). Particular thanks go to those who allowed me to use them as an example for this book.

Thanks also to Kate Williams for her patience and support in the writing of this little book and to colleagues who agreed to be my 'critical friends' for their supportive comments and sensible suggestions. Thanks to my colleagues at Oxford Brookes for their continued encouragement; in particular, to Lorraine Collett for her enthusiasm and ideas for this edition. Finally, a special thanks to my daughter Sallie for her witty and perceptive illustrations which enliven the series.

The author and publisher wish to thank the following for permission to reproduce copyright material: Houghton Mifflin Company, R. David Middlebrook, University of Hull, Mercier Press, Genius Within and Westminster School.

# Introduction

It takes enormous effort for students with dyslexia or other SpLDs (specific learning differences) to keep up with their studies at university. Most know dyslexia/SpLD involves memory and organisational problems but do not take up the one-to-one support they may be entitled to. As a dyslexic/SpLD student, you may not realise that understanding your SpLD means YOU can manage your SpLD positively and so work with it, not against it.

This little book is about understanding there is a dyslexic/SpLD learning style and using this to think about how to tackle a task before starting it. This will reduce your workload and increase your efficiency. It should also reduce the stress so many dyslexic/SpLD students experience and the impact of your SpLD/dyslexia on your studies.

Strategies are suggested throughout the book to work with your learning style. It is hoped you will try these out and use any you find useful. Please discard any that don't work for you. After reading this book, you should be able to consider what else you could use that would fit in with your own learning style.

*It is all about finding out what works for you and doing it your way!*

# How to use this guide

This guide does not need to be read all at once. Just keep coming back to it for ideas from time to time.

Part 1 explains why dyslexia/SpLD makes studying harder and gives ideas about how to work *with* your dyslexia/SpLD and not against it. This puts YOU in charge of your dyslexia/SpLD, not the other way round.

Part 2 concentrates on individual skills such as reading, writing and dealing with information. These can be read in any order – just dip in and out as needed.

Part 3 provides some information on what support should be available to you at university. It is worth looking at this if you are (or suspect you are) dyslexic or have another SpLD.

# PART 1

# IT IS OK TO DO THINGS DIFFERENTLY

The main message of this book is that IT IS OK to do things differently. You may have tried working in the same way as your friends – maybe taking notes in a lecture or working at the last minute through the night only to find that you don't understand what you have written. It is likely that these methods just don't seem to work for you. Give yourself permission to explore ways of working that will use your dyslexia/specific learning difference (SpLD) constructively.

## Dyslexia

Being dyslexic does not mean you are not as bright as other people – just that you learn differently. You can be clever and have an SpLD; your dyslexia or other SpLD does not determine your intelligence.

Famous dyslexics include Steve Redgrave, Kara Tointon, Eddie Izzard, Jamie Oliver, Keira Knightley, Steven Spielberg, Paloma Faith, Cher and even Walt Disney. Daniel Radcliffe has dyspraxia and Justin Timberlake has ADHD.

It is reckoned that 10% of students are dyslexic, so you are in good company.

What is dyslexia? A simple question, but one there has been much debate about. It is not important for you to understand everything about dyslexia, and every dyslexic person is unique, but you will share some characteristics.

## Characteristics of dyslexia

▶ short-term memory (or working memory) is not as efficient as that of non-dyslexics
▶ speed of processing information is slower than for non-dyslexics.

The good news is that your long-term memory is likely to be very good: once you have learnt something you really get it.

## Why all this matters

Simply put, it takes you much longer to process and remember information. This is why you are allowed extra time in exams and why it takes you ages to research and write your assignments.

These memory and processing difficulties mean your phonological knowledge (knowing how groups of letters represent sounds and the ability to put these together accurately) is not as developed as that of other learners. Reading and writing is not automatic or fluent for you. Comprehension of text is affected and spelling may also be erratic.

The same difficulties that affect reading and writing also affect organisation skills. These include managing time, organising ideas and structuring assignments.

## Dyslexia is *not the only* SpLD

Dyslexia is the most common SpLD but today it is recognised that it is not the only one. Next most common is dyspraxia, also called developmental coordination disorder (DCD).

## Can I have more than one SpLD?

Yes, it is now known that there is a high co-morbidity rate between SpLDs. This means that some SpLDs may overlap. It is estimated that half the population with dyslexia may also have dyspraxia/DCD (Kaplin 1998, cited by the Dyspraxia Foundation 2013). You may be really interesting and have other combinations of SpLDs.

'Neurodiversity' is a term used to explain the range of learning differences and includes dyslexia, dyspraxia, ADHD, ASD and dyscalculia. The important point for you if you have more than one SpLD is to understand the impact this may have on your learning style. The following diagram shows these can overlap and the strengths you may have with these conditions.

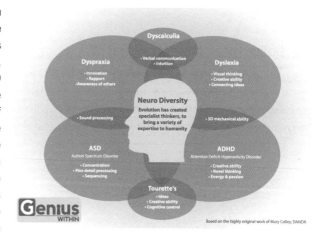

Source: Genius Within (2013). Based on a model by Mary Colley of DANDA (2006). www.geniuswithin.co.uk/infographics-and-literature/neuro-diversity-venn-diagram/.

For a more detailed model of this, see: www.achieveability.org.uk/files/1275491669/neuro-diversity-diagram.pdf.

A brief explanation of other common SpLDs is given below. This little book is too small to cover these in detail but do look at other books and websites. See also Useful resources at the end of this book.

## Characteristics of dyspraxia/DCD

Dyspraxia impacts at a cognitive level (thinking and organising thought) and on everyday physical activities such as writing, driving, team games and making meals (Kirby 2013). If you have dyspraxia, you will notice it takes a great deal of effort to keep yourself organised, your work well structured and computer files and paperwork in order. The good news is that unless you also have dyslexia, your reading and writing skills should be OK. It is the selection, sequencing and organisation of work you have to pay more attention to.

It can be very tiring and stressful to constantly be dealing with the consequences of forgetting, misplacing and losing things. Increasing stress causes more disorganisation. As a dyspraxic student, you need to understand you *will* be dealing with the *organisation issue daily and the resulting stress this causes*.

If your diagnosis is **dyspraxia/DCD only**, the following chapters will be helpful:

If you **also have dyslexia**, the *reading, writing and organisation* chapters will also be important to focus on.

All study skills advice that helps students with SpLD is, of course, useful for any student, so do dip in and out of the book.

# Characteristics of attention deficit (hyperactivity) disorder (ADD/ADHD)

Attention and concentration issues leading to restlessness and impulsivity. This results in planning and organisation difficulties. The sections on organisation, timekeeping and planning may help. Further sources of support can be found at the end of the book.

# Characteristics of autism spectrum disorder (ASD) and Asperger's syndrome

Social and communication issues. Further sources of support can be found at the end of this book.

# Characteristics of dyscalculia

Mathematical-type difficulties, severe non-recognition of mathematical scale and concepts, not simply a dislike of maths. Rather rare. Further sources of support can be found at the end of this book.

## Dyslexia: understanding short-term (working) memory – and why it matters!

It is necessary to learn a little more about short-term (or working memory) and speed of processing information to understand how you can learn effectively.

### Why this matters

It takes much more effort for dyslexics to learn NEW information. The only sure way is to **overlearn** material by going over and over it until you know it perfectly. All students learn this way, but it is much more important for dyslexic students, who cannot rely on learning quickly or at the last minute.

OVERLEARNING means reviewing your work OFTEN

## Understanding information processing – and why it matters!

You probably knew your short-term memory is not as good as your friends'. The other characteristic of dyslexia – slow information processing speed – may be new to you.

### Speed of information processing

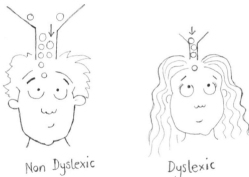

Non Dyslexic

Dyslexic

### Why this matters

Just when you need to deal with lots of information, say in a lecture, your speed of processing clogs up. This makes it almost impossible to listen *and* take notes, or, when you are reading, to comprehend *and* remember information.

Try to process a LITTLE information at a time

Work *with* your short-term memory by reviewing your stuff OFTEN – this is called 'overlearning'. Avoid information overload by limiting how much information you process: work for short bursts of time. Then you process a LITTLE at a time.

Drip-feed knowledge a LITTLE at a time and do this OFTEN!

Think of this like filling a glass. We can either:

slowly fill the glass by dripping water in

Or we can:

fill it too fast and find some of it splashing back out again

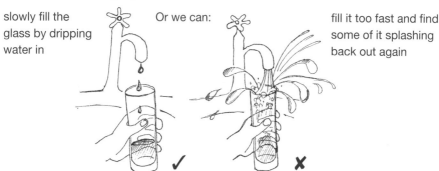

> **LITTLE and OFTEN – an effective dyslexic learning style**
> **Overlearning and working for short periods of time works best**

## Working out your personal learning style

Your **personal learning style** is a combination of:

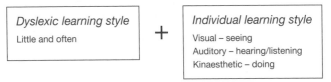

*Dyslexic learning style*

Little and often

+

*Individual learning style*

Visual – seeing
Auditory – hearing/listening
Kinaesthetic – doing

Knowing **which type of learner** you are allows you to adapt how you learn. If you are an auditory (verbal) learner, for example, using coloured mind maps may be a waste of time. If you learn by listening, it would be better to discuss your work with a friend, listen to recordings of notes, or use 'text-to-speech software' to have an article read to you.

If you do not know your individual learning style, try googling VAK (which stands for 'visual, auditory and kinaesthetic'). You should soon find a questionnaire to do online.

 Use your personal learning style and find out what works best for YOU

## Metacognition – or thinking about thinking

Metacognition means thinking about the processes involved when learning so that you understand how you learn best. This allows you to take control of organising your learning, monitoring your progress and achieving goals (Rose 2009).

Research (Torgesen 1981) shows that dyslexics find it hard to work out what a task involves and the best way to tackle it. Each new task is seen as a new problem and strategies already learned are not always applied.

This book is based on metacognition. It is about understanding how you learn and using strategies to become more effective in your work.

The aim is to end up with a reduced workload, which should also reduce stress. This is a bonus as the impact of dyslexia is usually worse when you are under stress.

# Working *with* other SpLDs

## Dyspraxia

The first step is to recognise that disorganisation is part of you. It won't go away and will be a daily challenge. However, being aware of this means that you can start to develop strategies to minimise the impact of dyspraxia. This does take effort but strategy building is the key to success.

Packing your bag the night before and using technology to send you reminders are a start. Contact your university SpLD support team to find out what one-to-one study skills and/or mentoring support is available to you. See the Useful contacts and Useful resources at the end of this book.

## Autism spectrum disorder (ASD) and Asperger's syndrome

The main issues are understanding the rules of social communication, which may affect communicating with staff and other students. Strengths include the ability to focus for long periods of time (Autistica 2014). Autistic people often have a unique view of the world, which can be interesting and valuable (National Autistic Society 2016).

Support is available at university through the Disabled Students' Allowance and may provide mentoring to assist with the transition to university life, communication and social skills, managing time and organisation. Do contact your university's Wellbeing or Student Support Service to see what is offered.

## Attention deficit (hyperactivity) disorder (ADD/ADHD)

Sitting through lectures may be hard and you may be allowed to leave them if you are experiencing difficulties. Your tutors will be made aware of this by your university's SpLD team. Use any lecture capture, slides and information on your uni's virtual learning environment to catch up.

Find out about and take up any specialist study or mentoring support available to you to help you keep on track. The ADHD & You website (www.adhdandyou.co.uk) has some useful tips for adults. See also Useful contacts and Useful resources at the end of this book.

## Dyscalculia

Difficulties with understanding and using mathematical concepts mean it may be problematic to pass compulsory maths tests, such as drug calculations for healthcare students and the professional numeracy skills test for new teachers. Many courses have 'hidden maths', which you may not have anticipated, and research often requires an understanding of statistics.

The British Dyslexia Association has an online document: www.bdadyslexia.org.uk/common/ckeditor/filemanager/userfiles/Dyscalculia_resources.pdf, which includes a comprehensive list of software and online interventions/programmes.

# STUDY SKILLS AT UNIVERSITY

## Skills needed at university

University is different from your previous learning experiences and you need to develop particular skills to help you study independently.

This part shows how you can improve these skills by using your individual learning style (visual, auditory or kinaesthetic) and your dyslexic/SpLD learning style. For dyslexia, this is using LITTLE and OFTEN. For dyspraxia, it is a focus on organisation and time management skills (see Chapters 4 and 5).

For other SpLDs, please see Useful contacts and Useful resources at the end of this book.

# Skills needed for university

organisation

note taking

writing

research

time management

groupwork

exams

lectures & seminars

presentations

dealing with information

reading

# Using assistive technology (AT) to help

Assistive technology can help with organisation, reading, note taking, planning, researching, writing and checking work.

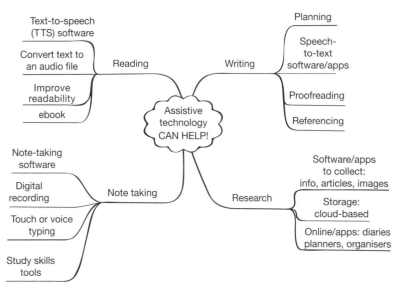

Students receiving DSA (Disabled Students' Allowance) funding may get a computer with assistive software. This usually includes mind mapping software and text-to-speech software. Most students do not realise how useful AT is. The DSA currently (2017) pays for training to use the software, so make sure you use it! Training videos are usually available with the software and on the suppliers' webpages. Do browse through these so you can learn how the software can help you.

Some universities have site licences for AT – useful if you are not eligible for DSA funding.

Also look for apps and software, some free:

▶ Diversity and Ability (DnA) is an excellent resource with an extensive range (www.dnamatters.co.uk/resources/). It lists what is available, what it can do, and links you straight to the webpage so you can download it. There are also links to videos explaining how to use the resources if these are available

▶ Wyvern Training Portal (https://users.wyvernportal.co.uk/courses/main-videos) offers free help videos on how to use assistive technology

▶ yourDSA (www.yourdsa.com) has a list of available assistive technology and links to software and apps (some free).

Some software suppliers offer free (limited day) downloads.

# 4   Organisation

The characteristics of *dyslexia* (slow information processing speed and short-term memory) also cause problems with **organisation.** If you are *dyspraxic*, personal organisation and keeping track of possessions and documentation are a daily challenge. Other SpLDs such as autism spectrum disorder may also experience issues with this, so this chapter is for everyone.

Organisation includes juggling time, work, family and social life, daily living tasks, academic tasks, and even structuring assignments.

Unless you can really rely on your memory, some sort of organising tool is a must. Take your pick from the table on the next page. Use one from each time zone.

| Time zone | Consider using | Comments |
|-----------|----------------|----------|
| Semester | Semester planner, wall planner, online calendar, mobile phone, task management apps such as Google Keep | Make a note of coursework type (essay, presentation), day due, % worth of total marks |
| Week | Online calendar, diary, timetable, 'to do' list (paper or apps), task management | Colour code different activities so you can see them at a glance – easy to do with apps |
| Day | 'To do' list (paper or app), diary, calendar, timetable, Stickies or Post-it notes | These can be on computer, a notebook, smartphone or anything you actually use |

*It does not matter what you use – just don't rely on your wobbly memory!*

*Extensions: DON'T unless the situation looks completely lost. You will only pay for it later – and have less time for other coursework or exam revision.*

# Organisation: how will you deal with the paperwork?

Not everything can be stored on the computer (PC), so you need a system to deal with all the paper you collect. Do this before you have other things to worry about – exams, for example.

Make sure you have files, dividers, plastic wallets and a hole punch. Consider doing the following.

**Files:**

▸ Colour code course files – a different colour for each study unit.

▸ Keep course files in your room and have one file you take into uni/college (use dividers for different units). Every week or so, review and file your notes in the course files.

▸ Use a separate file or box file for each piece of coursework so you can keep all the resources for it together.

**Notes:**

- Lecture notes: write course name/code, date and number on *every* page.
- From reading: record as much of the reference as you can.

 Pick a time once a week when you review, check and file paperwork – set your alarm in your mobile!

## Computer filing

Just because your documents are on the PC does not mean they don't need organising and filing.

Get into the habit of:

- creating folders for each new course unit/module
- having subfolders for reading/research, notes, assignments etc.
- colour coding or star folders to help find stuff quickly
- using consistent file names and dating to find latest version, such as Diabetes essay 22 Oct 17.doc or Diabetes essay 3.doc.

## Online storage

It is an excellent idea to store files in the 'cloud' so they can be accessed anywhere you can get online.

They can:

▶ be uploaded to the cloud from your PC
  ▶ Word docs, PowerPoint and Excel
  ▶ use folders, colour code or 'star' these
  ▶ share documents/files, a great idea for collaborative groupwork
    – be aware of possible plagiarism issues
    – anyone you share a folder with will be able to see ALL the files and subfolders within that folder. **Be sure you meant to do this!**
▶ be easily downloaded from the cloud into Word docs. Try Dropbox, Google Drive, Evernote, Google Keep.

For other ideas, do take a look at Diversity and Ability (DnA) at www.dnamatters.co.uk/resources/. This is an excellent resource with lists, explanations of use, searchable categories, links to webpages and videos.

For ANY type of storage, it is a good idea to *download occasionally* on to your PC or USB pen drive; and upload to the cloud or even print off a copy every now and then.

Time management is an issue for all students but can be especially difficult if you are also dealing with an SpLD. For dyspraxic students, this is a major issue and is also troublesome for dyslexics and students with autism.

If you are dyslexic, you will have noticed it takes you longer to do tasks than other students. In a seminar or lecture, you may not be able to finish reading something in the time allowed. When studying alone, you may not be aware just how much time you are taking over some activities. There is a big difference in the time you *estimate* a task will take and the *actual* time you spent doing it.

**Help yourself by noticing where the time goes:**
1 Think of a task you have done recently – maybe reading a chapter of a book or reviewing your notes.
2 Note down the total time it took to do (**actual** time).
3 How much time did you think it would take (**estimated** time)?
4 Putting it in a table may help you see which activities take most time.

## Estimated time vs Actual time

| Task | Estimated time (ET) | Actual time (AT) |
|------|---------------------|------------------|
| Breakfast | 10 mins | All morning |
| Reading – Ch. 2 sociology book | 2 hours | 5 hours |
| Reviewing notes for week 1 | Half hour | 3 hours |
| Your example | | |

This exercise helps identify which activities take more time than you realised.

Aim to use the **estimated** time only and adapt how you do the task to fit this. For example, use the Start and End reading method ( pp. 75–79 ) for the **estimated time only**, then stop. When reviewing notes, spend a minute or two per page only (see the Cornell note-taking system, pp. 47–49 ) or use Stickies/Post-it notes to summarise.

## Notice when you work best

Spend a few minutes now considering when you are at your best to work. This could save you hours of wasted effort.

These are Oli's best and worst working times.

| Early morning | Morning | Lunchtime | Early afternoon | Late afternoon | Evening | Late evening |
|---------------|---------|-----------|-----------------|----------------|---------|--------------|
| No way! | ? | Yes | No | Yes | No | Yes |

What are yours? Fill in the table.

| Early morning | Morning | Lunchtime | Early afternoon | Late afternoon | Evening | Late evening |
|---------------|---------|-----------|-----------------|----------------|---------|--------------|
| | | | | | | |

| Tasks to do when alert | Tasks to do when less alert |
|---|---|
| Reading, searching databases, taking notes from reading | Shopping, organising notes, finding books, eating, exercising, reviewing last week's notes, starting a reference list |
| Add your thoughts here: | Add your thoughts here: |

## How long can you work effectively for?

How long is it before you get distracted when working? 10 minutes? 20 minutes? Less? More? This will, of course, depend on the activity you are doing.

Dyslexia means you quickly become overloaded with information. Your brain tries to protect you by daydreaming or even dozing off. It is best to STOP before this happens, if you can.

Learn to recognise when you are working effectively (and when you are not). STOP as soon as you are getting distracted as this indicates you are becoming overloaded. Take a short break (or change to a lighter activity).

Vicky, a Social Care student, said:

*'I can't believe how my 10-minute rule has changed everything. I even stop my friends going on by putting my hand up and saying, "Sorry 10 mins up – I am not receiving!"'*

Vicky realised she concentrates quite well for up to 10 minutes. Then her attention drifts off. Now Vicky notices when this happens and cuts short any activities (even conversations!). This means she is working *with* her dyslexia, not against it. She is being effective by recognising when she is being ineffective.

Working for lots of short periods of time is much better than sitting down for two hours but only actually working effectively for 20 minutes of this. The graphs below illustrate how building in lots of breaks really will increase your effectiveness.

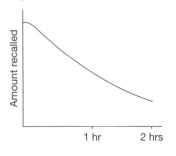
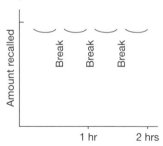

# If you are dyspraxic

Try the techniques above but if you are dyspraxic, time management is likely to be an even harder issue for you than for dyslexics, and even trickier if you have both conditions. You may find it hard to multitask and work better tackling one task at a time, which can be hard to achieve when you have lots of assignment guidelines at once.

**Prepare for tomorrow today**
Try packing your bag the night before. Put anything needed into one place or a box by the front door. This helps you review what you need to do tomorrow and have confidence that all is ready so less is likely to go wrong. Also, if anything has been missed, you have a bit of time to tackle it.

**Use a 'master' planner tool**
This is one place where everything is and kept up to date. It is easy to have odd bits of information everywhere, especially today with messages, mobiles, social media etc. Your master planner can be physical (a wallchart) or virtual (online calendar/diary). Up to you, but it must be **used and kept up to date**. If you find you are not doing this, consider another method (first try changing mode to physical or virtual).

**Keep going if it is going well**
It can be hard to restart after breaks (unlike dyslexics), so it is probably a good idea to keep going (Kirby 2013). Do stop though if you think the quality of what you are doing is falling.

# Time management tips for everyone

### Arranging meetings

Groupwork can fall apart if you fail to meet up regularly; try using doodle.com to get everyone together.

### Avoiding distractions

Today, it is harder than ever to avoid the distractions of the internet, social media and game playing, especially as you will be using your computer/smartphone constantly for research and writing up assignments.

Try website blockers and self-control apps, there are plenty available; for example, StayFocused is a Google Chrome extension.

### Fun to do lists

Try Google Keep. Or how about Habitica.com, which uses game-playing motivation techniques to help you complete tasks. Do solo or compete with friends.

There are plenty of to do list, task management and increasing productivity apps; you just need to find one you actually use.

## Dealing with information with dyslexia and/or dyspraxia

Dealing with information is your biggest challenge as a dyslexic and/or dyspraxic student at university or college. Most dyslexic/dyspraxic students are aware that they work much harder than their friends without an SpLD and are not always rewarded with the grades they think they deserve. Dyslexia affects how well you can process information, and your short-term memory means it takes time to learn effectively. Given time, you can deal with information effectively. If you are dyspraxic, you may be able to process information efficiently but the issue is how to organise or use it.

You have a choice:

**either**
you can just carry on trying to do everything, which will lead to you becoming increasingly exhausted as the year continues

**or**
you can take steps to reduce your workload and become more efficient.

# How to start reducing your workload

Previously, you have been directed to the information needed for your courses and provided with notes, handouts and the required reading. University is different. Lectures and seminars provide the main ideas and themes to consider, but then it is up to you to find out more for yourself.

You'll have to learn the best way for YOU to process the information from:

| Lectures | Reading lists | Course information |
|---|---|---|
| Seminars | Research | VLE (virtual learning environment) |

It is easy to become overwhelmed by the sheer volume of information. However, you can help yourself a lot if you begin by considering *why* you have been set a task – your tutor will have had a *purpose* in mind. Then you need to choose a way to tackle the task that fits with this purpose.

## Identifying your purpose

| Task | Purpose | Why | Which means | Strategy |
|------|---------|-----|-------------|----------|
| **1** Pre-reading for lecture | Prepare for lecture | Pick up main ideas – fast | Don't need detailed reading | Read the abstract, the introduction and conclusion, then headings/subheadings |
| **2** Revision of subject | Fill in the gaps | Complete knowledge | Only do the bits you don't know | List the areas not yet tackled. Do in order of importance |
| Your example | | | | |

**1** Reading *all* the suggested pre-reading in detail would take ages. However, if you choose to apply the Start and End reading method ( pp. 75–79 ), you will get the main ideas without deep reading the whole chapter or article. By fitting what you did to the purpose, you have reduced your workload.

**2** Revising only the bits you have not covered before (filling in the gaps) helps target your revision so you don't waste time on things you already know well.

This is using metacognition to think about the PURPOSE first and then using this to pick a suitable STRATEGY – so you only do the work that is **actually needed.**

Making informed choices like this puts YOU in charge – and increases your efficiency.

 Before starting a task, consider what the PURPOSE is and WHY it was set

# Virtual learning environment

Your university will have a virtual learning environment (VLE). This is a web-based resource that can be accessed when you are off-site. Do go hunting around it: your tutors will assume you have looked at any material they put on the VLE.

| Advantages | But you may |
|---|---|
| All your course information will be there, such as assignments, assessment criteria, lecture PowerPoint slides and maybe videos of lectures, discussion forums | Not know what is on it |
| You cannot lose it! | Dislike working on the PC |
| It may have other resources your tutors think are useful | Lack confidence in your IT skills |
| Your one-to-one specialist support tutor can see any course guidance you have | Not get around to reading it, although tutors will assume you have |

VLEs are an invaluable resource. Make sure you can access and use yours

## Your course information

Your course handbook is essential reading! It should tell you:

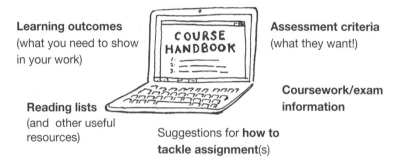

**Learning outcomes**
(what you need to show
in your work)

**Assessment criteria**
(what they want!)

**Reading lists**
(and other useful
resources)

**Coursework/exam
information**

Suggestions for **how to
tackle assignment**(s)

## Lectures at university

Lectures are the main point of contact between teaching staff and students at
university. They provide a foundation or starting point for your studies.

So, you can expect to study independently for many hours outside the time spent in
lectures.

**A course unit** may have **150 hours** total study time – but only **30 hours** contact time, so **120 hours** are independent study time. You will have three or four separate courses, so this is a lot of individual study!

Practical or scientific subjects require more contact time in university as you will also have practical or laboratory sessions. Arts subjects such as History or English may have very little time spent in lectures or seminars.

Knowing this can help you put lectures in perspective: their main PURPOSE is to open up the possibilities or main ideas associated with that subject, not to provide everything you need to know.

Attendance at lectures is important as you'll find out what you should focus on for your course, but it may not be necessary for you to record everything the lecturer says.

 At university, lectures are just the starting point for your studies

# Note taking in lectures

Dyslexic and dyspraxic students both have difficulties with taking notes.

Most *dyslexic* students try hard to take notes in lectures, but find that they can EITHER follow what is being said OR take notes, but not BOTH!

For *dyspraxic* students, handwriting may be a major issue, making notes difficult to read and organisation of notes chaotic.

Ask yourself: *What do I do with my lecture notes?*

Answer the question honestly; it makes a difference to how you deal with note taking in lectures.

If this is you:

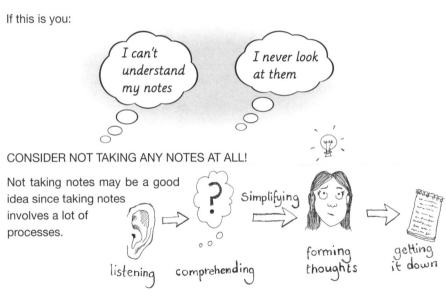

CONSIDER NOT TAKING ANY NOTES AT ALL!

Not taking notes may be a good idea since taking notes involves a lot of processes.

Doing all this requires quick processing and good memory skills. These are not dyslexic strengths, so note taking in lectures works against your dyslexic learning style.

You may understand more by concentrating on what is said and restricting any notes taken to main ideas, names of theorists and any references given so you can look them up later. Check if lectures will be recorded and available for you to view later on your uni's VLE.

**If you decide not to take notes, before the lecture, consider:**

**1 How will you keep focused?**

Suggestions include:

- recording the lecture
- using note-taking software or apps
- ticking off where you are on any notes provided
- doodling (can help you focus on what is being said)
- creating diagrams, mind maps, keywords for any resources mentioned.

**2 How will you review the lecture material?**

Suggestions include:

- immediately afterwards writing down everything you can recall
- going for coffee with a friend and discussing the lecture
- finding suggested reading (see course information)
- following up information on handouts – and adding in new notes
- asking your subject librarian to help find sources.

# Unhelpful strategies you may have to change

In your previous learning you were probably given lots of notes and didn't really need to do much research outside this. University is different because you have to develop knowledge and understanding beyond your lecture materials.

Try to avoid doing the following, as they are a waste of time and effort:

▶ **copying out notes**: it is not possible to keep up with the volume of rewriting and this will prevent you developing your knowledge *outside* that presented in the lecture.

▶ **worrying about neat notes**: the only requirement for your notes is that you understand them. They are a working document and do not need to be neat. They are for your eyes only.

▶ **trying to write down everything:** this will only result in notes you don't understand. Make as brief notes as you can. You may be given handouts, which you can add brief notes to.

You could **change your strategy**. If you are still doing any of the above, think how you could adapt this and save time. Maybe you could record thoughts from your notes on a digital recorder or mind map, or reduce these onto Stickies/Post-it notes. These are all quicker than rewriting.

# Tips that work when you have to take notes

**Avoid taking notes**
Just note down where you can find the information later on, plus key information such as names of researchers and theories.

**Preview any notes available**
Do this *before* the lecture if possible. This works because it allows you to process more information in the actual lecture. Just knowing the format of the lecture in advance helps (you'll notice when the lecturer goes off track!).

**Reduce amount of notes you take**
Always ask the lecturer for notes. Even better, ask them to put them up on your uni's VLE (and *before* the lecture if possible). Can you photocopy someone else's notes?

**Use your learning style**
Decide what method of note taking may work for you:

**Visual** learner            use mind mapping, highlighting, coloured pens
**Auditory** learner        record notes and listen again later
**Kinaesthetic** learner    type notes using a laptop, mind mapping

# Note-taking systems: selecting what works for you

There are two basic note-taking systems:

Linear      or      mind mapping

1 Importance of fair tests
  - sciences is...
  - A Challenging
2 How fair tests take
  children's ...
  - Ref to construc ...
  - etc.
3 Analyse the process....
  - Good lesson LO
  - Subject knowledge
  - etc

Arrabella (Primary
Teacher Education)

You can choose whichever one you are more comfortable with – or mix and match.
Not *all* dyslexics like mind mapping! Dyspraxics may prefer mind mapping as it suits
their 'grasshopper' brain, jumping from one thought to another, but there are no rules,
so do whichever you prefer.

## Other useful note-taking strategies

Technology has transformed the way we can record information with:

Record

Note taker-
only if recommended

Smart pen

Touch typing

You may have had some of this recommended in your assessment. If supplied, do make sure you take up any training on how to use it. Otherwise, there are free recording software and apps available. See Diversity and Abilities (DnA) for comprehensive listing of useful software and apps (www.dnamatters.co.uk/resources/).

### Lecture capture

Many universities now use lecture capture to record lectures and if so it will be available on your VLE. Do be aware, however, that the lectures are only a starting point for your research.

### Digital recorders

Record lectures and load up recorded Dictaphone audio notes. These can be edited, named and filed in folders. You may have this supplied through DSA but if not there are apps available. See: www.dnamatters.co.uk/resources/reviews/digital-voice-recorders/.

### Note-taking software

Audio examples available as software/apps include Audio Notetaker, Notetalker and AudioNote. These allow you to visualise your audio recordings. You can personalise them by adding colour, text, images, photos and PowerPoint slides. You can also add time stamps so you can return to interesting points, organise your notes and search for keywords (Simpson 2016).

Notability allows you to make quick notes and annotate pdfs and lectures slides.

Take a browse around app stores for one that suits you.

Smartpens can record lecture notes for replay. They usually require specialist notepaper, although a good quality printer can reproduce usable notepaper.

**Whatever note-taking system you are using, do remember to record:**

▶ Date (or week of course)
▶ Course name (or choose a 'course' colour and mark top of paper with this)
▶ Topic
▶ Page number (on every page please!).

Doing this for **EVERY** lecture *will help with the filing* later!

## The Cornell note-taking system (or two-column system)

If and when you have to take notes, select a note-taking system that works for you. Certainly try mind mapping or recording lectures, but there may be times when using a linear-type system works. The Cornell note-taking system works well with the dyslexic learning style (LITTLE and OFTEN) as it has features that promote reviewing and revisiting your notes, which assists your learning process.

**Method for Cornell note taking:**

▶ **During the lecture:** Record (brief) notes in the right-hand Notes column.
▶ **After the lecture:** Fill in the Summary box (after 24 hours or so). Note the main points. Be creative with colour, drawings, mini mind map, keywords or bullet points.

▶ **Later on:** Fill in the Review column – add questions, keywords, theory names, references, or build up an index so you can review your notes easily.

 Reviewing notes means you are actively working with them and also memorising them!

Divide an A4 sheet of paper and use as below.

| Review column | Notes |
|---|---|
| Up to 1/3rd of page width | Up to 2/3rd of page width |
| **Summary** 2" or about 7 lines | |

| Review column | Notes |
|---|---|
| Use for:<br><br>Questions,<br><br>Keywords<br><br>Index | Take notes as usual, be brief, avoid sentences |
| **Summary** Shortly after the lecture, list, bullet point or mind map the most important points from your notes here. | |

## The Cornell note-taking system: going deeper

The full version of the Cornell note-taking system suggests that you:

| Record | Take notes using keywords/bullet points. Keep it brief! |
|---|---|
| Question | Write any questions you have in the Review column; this may be any gaps or anything you don't understand |
| Recite | Look at questions and keywords. Say out loud what you can recall |
| Reflect | Ask reflective questions:<br>▶ What's the significance of these facts?<br>▶ What principle are they based on?<br>▶ How can I apply them?<br>▶ How do they fit in with what I already know?<br>▶ What's beyond them? |
| Review | Spend time each week to browse through your notes. Focus on the Summary and Review column to start with |

*Source*: Adapted from Pauk (2001).

For more information and examples of Cornell and mind mapping note-taking systems see: http://theconversation.com/whats-the-best-most-effective-way-to-take-notes-41961.

Here is a mind map to show how assistive technology can help with note taking.

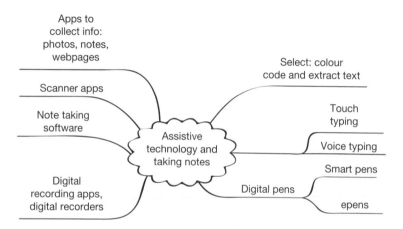

Apps to collect info: photos, notes, webpages

Scanner apps

Note taking software

Digital recording apps, digital recorders

Assistive technology and taking notes

Select: colour code and extract text

Touch typing

Voice typing

Digital pens

Smart pens

epens

## Before you rush off to collect resources

It is a huge temptation to rush off to the library and collect as much information as you can. This is a mistake, especially if you are dyslexic.

You must **target** your research, or this might happen:

**Your research (an elephant amount) won't fit into a matchbox ('word count')!**

This is double (or even triple) trouble because you spent time finding the information, got confused as it *all* seemed so important, wrote it up, and finally spent hours cutting it down to fit your word count.

Word Count        Your Research

# What is difficult about researching for dyslexic/dyspraxic students?

Whether you are dyslexic or dyspraxic, research poses particular problems as it requires targeting your reading and organising the material found. One difference between these conditions when you are doing research is that dyslexics benefit from the LITTLE and OFTEN technique, whereas dyspraxics may find that it is helpful to keep going when things are going well (Patrick 2015).

Both dyslexic and dyspraxic students find it hard to:

- multitask, that is, research several assignments at once
- know when to stop researching and start writing
- keep track of references
- deal with library environments.

The advice in this chapter should help whatever your SpLD.

**Here is a model of your course:**

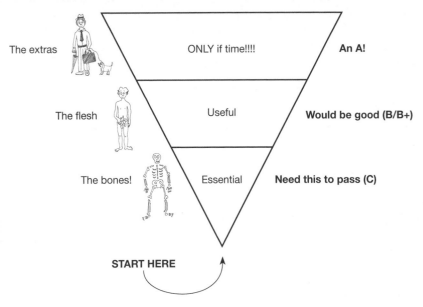

The extras — ONLY if time!!!! — **An A!**

The flesh — Useful — **Would be good (B/B+)**

The bones! — Essential — **Need this to pass (C)**

**START HERE**

| To achieve grade | You must ... |
|---|---|
| C – a pass | Cover the bottom triangle. This is the essential knowledge and understanding needed – the bones of the course |
| B – would be good | Include the important knowledge too – the bones fleshed out |
| A – only if time | Add the extra details, like clothes and accessories, but only if you have time! |

This fits in well with the dyslexic learning style of LITTLE and OFTEN, as each time you return to a subject you add a few more layers. You are doing the *overlearning process* that is essential to the dyslexic learning style.

## Ideally, this happens

You build up your knowledge and understanding from the essentials (a C) to the useful (a B) then – only if you have time – to an A with any extra detail.

$$C \longrightarrow B \longrightarrow A$$

Knowledge is built up a little at a time, working with your short-term memory and adding more detail each time – and working *with* your dyslexic learning style.

## But the dyslexic tendency is to do this in reverse, so

You try to do everything in the detail needed to get an A. This is hard enough without dyslexia, but add in the dyslexic difficulties of slow information processing speed and memory issues and you can see this is heading for trouble.

**A ⟶ B ⟶ C**

(try to avoid this)

This explains why you may get variable grades. If you are lucky and your essay or exam matches with the bits you did in detail, you get the A. Usually, though, this is a bit hit and miss. If bits of the essential stuff were skipped, you risk not doing so well. In extreme cases you may fail, despite knowing some of it to an A standard.

The key to this is **reducing your workload** so you can confidently apply the dyslexic learning style of LITTLE and OFTEN to different learning situations.

## Reduce your workload!

This is crucial to your success at university; you simply *must not* try to do everything. You need to think about how you tackle your learning – see metacognition (p. 14). This is vital if you are dyslexic, since it takes so much longer to research, read up, write and check assignments and revise for exams.

Starting university is rather like entering a race: you need to get to the finish line in the quickest time and go straight there, not wander around the track aimlessly or collapse long before you get there.

You could:

Try to do it all

OR

collect loads sort it later

OR

THINK how to tackle it

SO

reducing how much you have to do

Doing it all is exhausting and not effective in the end

Try these strategies:

| When | Try | If it goes wrong |
|------|-----|------------------|
| Reading | Ask: 'What do I need to find out?' Write it down and only do this. Questions and subquestions may help here | Note the reference of anything interesting; *briefly* note what it is. Now leave it alone! You have the reference if you need it for later |
| Researching | Ask yourself what you already know, then identify gaps. Target research carefully | If you find yourself randomly researching, try to see where the new information will fit in. If you can't, leave that topic for now |
| Writing | Frame and fill ( p. 96 ) | Map out a mini plan of what you could cover, then ✓, ✗ or ? ideas. Only use ticked bits for now. You can 'fill in' later |
| Revising | Prioritise topics. Look at past papers; some topics always come up | Too many areas to cover? Use Cornell method ( pp. 47–49 ). For notes already taken, use Stickies/Post-it notes to summarise. Start with the basics. Add detail later |

 Reducing what you research by keeping things simple will help

# Keep it simple – tips

Reduce the amount of information you have to deal with by recognising when you are overcomplicating your task, going off at a tangent or just doing too much detail. These are very dyslexic traits. Avoid unnecessary work:

▶ Start with the **basics** and **build** up to a full picture
▶ Recognise if you are an **overresearcher**
▶ Notice when you are **mind wandering.**

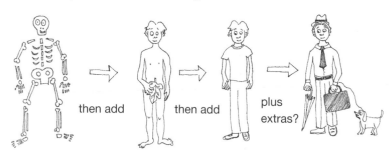

then add       then add       plus extras?

- **Basics first:** Build up your understanding, bit by bit. Think of this as starting with the skeleton and gradually adding layers.
- **Recognise if you are an overresearcher** (remember the elephant and matchbox; see p. 51): This stems from a lack of focus and insecurity about what you are being asked to do. Targeting what you need to research first will massively reduce your workload.
- **Notice mind wandering:** 'Mind wandering' can explain why you end up writing an essay that does not answer the question you were asked.

*Juan, a Fine Art student, wrote Van Gogh's complete life story when he was asked to analyse one of Van Gogh's paintings and say what this told the viewer about Van Gogh's state of mind. Juan realised that his passion about finding out more about Van Gogh took over. As a result, he failed.*

Browsing the internet makes mind wandering really easy! So be mindful and notice when this happens – you can waste a lot of time following false lines of enquiry. Keep asking yourself *why* you are doing a task and *where* what you are doing fits in.

**Doing research** 59

## Using the library

Libraries can be quite scary places, but remember they are not like supermarkets, which keep changing where things are on the shelves. Exerting a little effort early on to understand how the library works and where your subject area is will really benefit you.

Your library will do tours. Make sure you take one; sometimes, these can be virtual tours allowing you to prepare before you actually need the library.

Tips from students include:

Even 2nd or 3rd years can benefit from a tour, as technology changes all the time

Do a repeat tour if needed— no one will notice!

Get to know your subject librarian— they know where the resources for your subject are!

## Subject librarians are brilliant because they can:

 Do tell them you are dyslexic or have an SpLD and need to target your reading – or they may swamp you with information!

# What sort of information should I look for?

This, of course, depends on your subject, but there are some basic rules:

1 **Use reliable sources** that have been written by established academics in the field. These will have been peer reviewed and checked by other experts to make sure the material included is reliable.

2 **Use journals for up-to-date information**. It is important to know what the current developments in your field are. This is especially important in science and medical subjects where knowledge and practice change fast. *Unless it is an influential text, use sources less than 10 years old.*

**Academic books** are peer reviewed so usually reliable, but may not be up to date by the time they are published, **so use journals as well.**

## Databases

All universities subscribe to databases, which store thousands of online journals. It is *essential* you learn how to access and use these to get up-to-date resources. Look at your library information pages and if you get stuck, contact your subject librarian, explain you are dyslexic or have an SpLD and ask them to take you through the process.

## Critical thinking

Doing research is not simply collecting information. You need to actively do some critical thinking in order to come to some conclusions for yourself and your reader. This is crucial in order to gain good grades.

See www.nottingham.ac.uk/studentservices/documents/criticalthinkingmodelflyerhand outfromlearnhigher.pdf for a simple critical thinking model to help with this. Print both sides off and have it near to hand or on your wall for quick reference.

## Keyword searching

Databases are vast, so it can be hard to find what you are looking for. Simple keyword searches will throw up hundreds or thousands of results – or sometimes none!

Write down any words that spring to mind:
- use the computer synonyms finder or thesaurus
- use Google by typing your word and 'define' in the search bar to get alternative words and synonyms
- add new keywords you find in abstracts or journal articles (usually near the abstract).

**Boolean operators** AND, OR and NOT are useful to narrow or widen your search.

This example is from the Boolean Machine: http://rockwellschrock.com/rbs3k/boolean/index.htm.

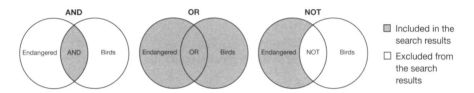

☐ Included in the search results

☐ Excluded from the search results

 **TOP TIP**

Missing off the end of a word – truncation – widens the search area. For example, using the keyword 'employ' will find 'employee', 'employer' and 'employment'. Some databases use * to indicate this, so enter the keyword employ* to get all the possible endings.

Do look at Dealing with Information ( pp. 33–50 ) and Organisation ( pp. 21–25 ) so you can keep on top of sorting out the research you have so carefully collected. Some software and apps can be very helpful for this.

## Using technology to help

### Collecting and storing resources

There are some great aids to keeping notes, photos, pdfs, record notes, collect online articles, to do lists, set reminders and more. Try Evernote, Google Keep, OneNote.

*Scanner apps* provide a quick way to record info for later; try Office Lens or Evernote Scannable.

**Back it up!** There is no excuse today for not saving your work. You have the options of saving it to the cloud, for example Google Drive, Dropbox or Boxifier (part of Dropbox that allows you to back up your My Documents folder to the cloud), memory stick, or just email it to yourself.

### Keep track of references

It does not matter how you do this, but just do it:

▶ save to favourites in databases or on your PC
▶ copy and paste the URL
▶ photograph or scan info using your smartphone
▶ Word has a useful referencing tab.

Some referencing apps and software let you email references to yourself, for example *Cite them right online*. Whatever you use, do check they fit with your uni's referencing style.

## Nobody reads everything!

Reading is acknowledged as an issue for most dyslexics. If you are dyspraxic, this may not be a particular issue for you unless you are also dyslexic. This section will look at why dyslexics experience difficulty with reading, analyse how *you* tackle reading, and offer a range of strategies for you to try. It starts with a basic reading strategy that fits with your dyslexic learning style, processing LITTLE, but doing this OFTEN.

Other ideas will be looked at that suit the different general learning styles (visual, auditory and kinaesthetic – VAK), so bear your individual learning style in mind. You can of course try any of the methods outlined.

No student reads everything on their reading list, however hard they may try. Keeping up with reading is an issue for many students, not just dyslexic ones.

 The trick for all readers is to mimic what effective readers do

## Why is reading hard for me? (Or why do I fall asleep when reading?)

Dyslexia is diagnosed when reading, writing and spelling skills are not as good as your ability suggests they should be (assuming there is not another explanation for this, such as missing education as a child). The assessment is likely to have shown that your working memory is weaker and your information processing speed is slower than for non-dyslexics.

As only a few words at a time can be held in your working memory, you may forget the beginning of the sentence by the time you get to the end of it. Academic texts can have long sentences, so this leads to lots of rereading.

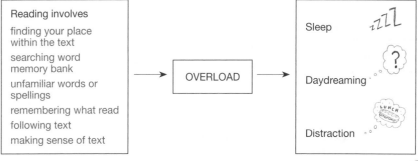

Reading involves
finding your place within the text
searching word memory bank
unfamiliar words or spellings
remembering what read
following text
making sense of text

→ OVERLOAD →

Sleep

Daydreaming

Distraction

## So how do I read?

Reading overloads the dyslexic brain so you end up rereading, not really understanding what you have read and probably dropping off after 10–20 minutes.

*So how do I read?* A quick analysis will reveal if you are working with your dyslexic learning style. Try this:

▶ Visualise the last text you read. After you selected the material, what did you do?
▶ Tick the responses that match best.

| What I did | ✓ or ✗ |
|---|---|
| Started at the beginning and read to the end | |
| Started but only got part way through | |
| Read it all but took ages and kept returning to it | |
| Read it all in one go | |
| Left it so late I didn't have time to read any of it | |
| Got distracted and didn't read it | |

**Anything else?** Did you understand it? Could you explain what the main point was in a couple of sentences without looking back at it? This is not a test, but just to get you to think about **how you tackle your reading**.

# What does my reading analysis tell me?

It tells you what you usually do without thinking! It is easy to start a task without considering why you are doing it, or what you want from it.

If you jump straight in and read everything from start to finish, you will soon be overloaded with information.

This causes:

Now for a bit of honesty. How long can you *really* read effectively without getting distracted or just reading the words without the information going in? 10 minutes? 15? 20? This will vary with the type of text you are reading, but try to think of this for **your usual course reading**.

This is the amount of time it is effective for YOU to read for.

I can read *effectively* for ........ minutes.

## So what do good readers do?

If you are dyslexic, reading *every* word in order is like looking at a building by examining every stone – it reveals very little. You need to stand back to get an overview first.

You can mimic what good readers do by looking at the shape of writing and selecting bits of the text to read, using *your* effective reading time.

# There are different types of reading: do these help?

Depending on the reading purpose, you may choose to:

Scan — *Looking for specific words/ keywords*

Skim — *Glancing over text for key ideas*

Deep read — *Close reading of the text to gain understanding*

- **Scanning** requires looking for a particular word in the text.
- **Skimming** involves processing lots of information (fast) and then trying to recall and sift out the important bits.
- **Deep reading** means trying to process information, recall what was written, understand this and link it to previously learnt material in your memory.

If these techniques work for you – use them.

**However,** many dyslexics find scanning, skimming and deep reading don't work. This is because they all put extra pressure on your weak processing speed and memory. This is where metacognition can help. Thinking about the *purpose* of what is being read determines the strategy used to approach it.

# Think before you start reading anything!

Researching for information and then reading it takes a lot of time for dyslexic students at university. Using metacognition and thinking about the purpose of your reading *before* you start will help you reduce the amount you read.

## Questions to ask before you start reading

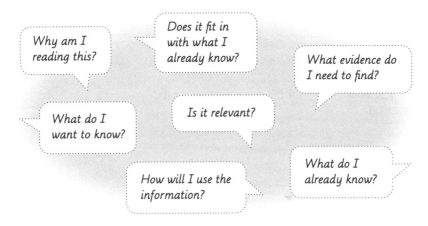

Why am I reading this?

Does it fit in with what I already know?

What evidence do I need to find?

What do I want to know?

Is it relevant?

What do I already know?

How will I use the information?

## Useful strategies to help stick to the purpose of your reading

### 1 QUADS

The QUADS grid may be useful to record information from your reading. QUADS stands for *Question, Answer, Detail, Source* (Rose Report, 2009).

| **QU**estion | **A**nswer | **D**etail | **S**ource |
|---|---|---|---|
| | | | |

### 2 SQ3R

SQ3R stands for *Survey, Question, Read, Recall* and then *Review* later. This method fits in well with the dyslexic learning style of LITTLE and OFTEN as it encourages you to revisit the text so helping with overlearning.

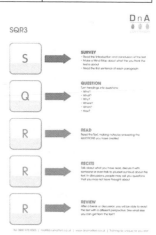

*Source:* DnA, www.dnamatters.co.uk/
resources/reviews/sqr3-handout/.

### 3 The Cornell note-taking system

*Record*, *Question*, then later on *Recite*, *Reflect* and *Review*. See pp. 47–49 for details.

Notice that all these techniques encourage thinking about what you want to find out before you waste valuable time just reading anything you find. It does not matter which strategy you use – as long as you ask yourself *why* you are reading something and *what* you need to find out before you start. All the systems also promote *reviewing* material, which is vital to the dyslexic learning style.

## Reading the start and the end

Skimming and scanning techniques are hard for dyslexics to do. It is very easy to start automatically deep reading – reading every word and processing all the information, whether needed or not.

The **Start and End** technique helps to get an overview of the text (the basics) by reading the first and last paragraphs and then adding to this by noting headings, subheadings, tables and diagrams. Finally, you select paragraphs to read and only deep read essential information. At every stage, you ask yourself: 'Do I really *need* to read this?'

Using the diamond shape of anything written ( p. 93 ) can save lots of time when reading.

*Stage 1*　　**Read the start and end only**

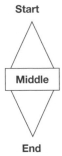

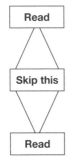

| **Start:** May include abstract, introduction, any learning outcomes, keywords, summary |
| :--- |
| **Skip the middle** |
| **Middle:** Writer goes into detail. STOP reading for now |
| **Go to the end** |
| **End:** May include summary, conclusion, key facts |

*Stage 2*　　**Flick through the middle**

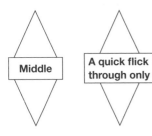

**Notice**

- Headings and subheadings
- Graphics – diagrams, tables, charts, graphs, figures
- Other types of info – case history, examples
- Any key points highlighted or mini summaries; look in margins or for boxes

### Stage 3    STOP: consider if you need to read any more

Now, you should have a fair idea of what the text is about – an overview. Write this down if you wish.

Get into the habit of asking yourself: 'Do I need to read more?' If the answer is no, leave it for now! It still exists, so you can decide to read more later on, but you may just have saved yourself time and effort by asking this question.

### Stage 4    Decide which sections you WILL read

Pick up a pencil (or use small Post-it notes) to mark what you will read. If it is your own copy of a book, it may help to lightly mark in the margin by the text:

✓       must read

✗       don't think needed

?       not sure

If you are using a library book, rub out any pencil marks you've made; or you could scan and print, photocopy or just mentally note which sections to skip.

This is what Catherine's article looked like after she did this (note: you only have to mark the text in the margins!):

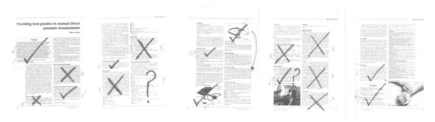

You can see now that Catherine has to read much less than she originally thought. This simple technique can reduce your reading load at a pencil stroke!

### Stage 5          *Ask yourself again: 'Do I need to read more?'*

Being selective will conserve your energy and work better with your dyslexic learning style.

### Stage 6          *Read the start of selected paragraphs*

By selectively reading the beginning of paragraphs, you will get the main idea. It will depend on your purpose whether you need to read the detail. Bear in mind that you may not need the precise detail anyway.

| Stage 7 | *Ask yourself again: 'Do I need to read more?'* |
| Stage 8 | *Only now consider reading the text in detail. This is DEEP READING* (see p. 72) |

Every paragraph should contain one idea that is developed. The first sentences usually indicate the main idea. Following sentences provide evidence, examples or arguments to support or dismiss the main idea.

Only deep read when you need detailed information. It takes time and effort and you may have to reread it several times before you understand it. Learn to be mindful about *when* you deep read and don't just automatically fall into deep reading.

When you decide to deep read, read the text in short chunks, stopping as soon as you get sleepy or distracted, as this indicates you are working beyond your memory and processing capacity. Take a break and come back to it later.

## Why the Start and End method is good for dyslexic readers

The Start and End method is effective because you use your maximum concentration time to learn a bit more depth each time you revisit the article. Doing this in short bursts means you start the process of overlearning, but do not overload your memory or processing capacity.

## Other reading strategies

Reading journals or chapters using the Start and End method fits in with the LITTLE and OFTEN dyslexia learning style, but you also have an individual learning style (VAK). There are other reading strategies that can make the most of your individual learning style.

| Learning style | Reading strategy |
|----------------|------------------|
| Visual | Use software that highlights text as it is read out; text-to-speech (TTS) software can do this (see below). Also try textmapping (see below) |
| Auditory | Convert text to a sound file using assistive technology (TTS software). Listen to recordings, downloads, read aloud or listen to someone reading aloud. Copy and paste text into TTS software (see below) |
| Kinaesthetic | Read aloud, listen to recording or download while doing something else – on the bus, exercising, walking |

## Using assistive technology to help with reading

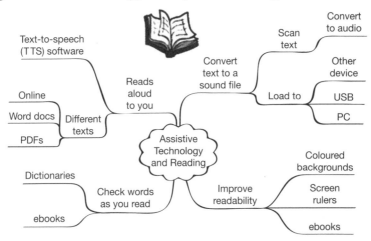

## Text-to-speech (TTS) software

TTS will read text aloud to you. Some packages will be supplied to students with DSA funding.

For non-funded students, alternatives include:

- NaturalReader
- Read&Write for Google Chrome
- ClaroRead
- Balabolka
- WordTalk for Windows.

You can listen to webpages:

- on browsealoud from texthelp.com
- Speak It is a Google Chrome extension app playable on any device.

## OCR (optical character recognition)

If your text is difficult to read, you can convert it to an electronic format using OCR. You can adapt it to your own preferences for font, background colour and use text-to-speech. Texthelp and ClaroRead can do this, as well as free RoboBraille and Google Keep (Batliwala et al. 2016).

## Ebooks

Many texts are now available as ebooks and your uni library will have these. With ebooks, you can adapt font size, background colour and line spacing. They have dictionaries and highlighting functions.

You can use ebooks on all devices including *ereaders* such as Kindle and Kobo (Batliwala et al. 2016).

## Textmapping

Textmapping helps visual and/or kinaesthetic learners to engage with the text in an interactive way (developed by R. David Middlebrook 1990):

**Photocopy or print** off the text onto single sided paper

**Join it all together** in one whole piece

**Map the text** using your own system of colours and notes. This encourages you to 'see' the text as a whole and not get stuck in the detail you will not remember in the middle.

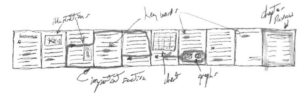

**Roll it up** and store as a scroll

Concentrate on beginnings and endings (introduction and conclusion); then starts and ends of sections to focus on the main ideas.

For more information on textmapping, see www.textmapping.org.

## Taking notes from reading

When making notes from reading, it is easy to start writing (or highlighting) too much. This is a sign you have fallen into deep reading.

Try not to make notes until after you have read the introduction and any conclusion (and abstract if there is one), using any of the reading strategies outlined (Start and End, textmapping, text to speech).

Then try to write:
▶ What you think the main idea is
▶ Why you think this is important
▶ How you can use it.

You may find it useful to do this at the top of any notes you make.

| Date | Notes |
|---|---|
| Full ref | |
| Find out | 1.<br>2.<br>3. |
| What about | After you have read the introduction, conclusion and abstract, write in 2–3 sentences what you think the writer's main point is |
| Why important | |
| What do I need to know? | |
| | Now you can start to take brief notes |
| Summary | Leave space to do this later |

Consider if you need to know anything else – go back to any questions you wrote down.

Find the answer to any new questions you think of. Write this down.

Any other questions?

# Using technology to help with note taking from reading

Use technology to 'voice' record information. Try using a 'voice typing' tool, such as in Read&Write, or Google 'voice typing' in Google Docs (under the Tools tab), and directly talk into the computer to type up your notes. Don't just read the material out though; read a passage, close the reference material and try to put the main idea into your own words so you demonstrate your learning. Remember to record the reference!

# Visual stress: using coloured backgrounds can help

Up to 40% of dyslexics may also experience visual stress (also called Meares–Irlen syndrome, scotopic sensitivity syndrome or visual dyslexia). If you find text is blurred, moves or the white spaces glare you may benefit from using coloured backgrounds when reading. This can reduce glare and increase concentration:

- For books: use coloured filters, overlays or tinted glasses
- For printed copies: try coloured paper; off-white and pale blue are popular choices
- For computer screens: change the display background or the colour of the font.

Try ClaroView, WindowShades or ScreenShades. Free f.lux software reduces glare and screen brightness according to the time of day. These measures may have a dramatic effect on your reading speed and comprehension, but do not work for everyone.

# Why is writing hard for me?
# (Or, I know it but can't get it down on paper)

Every dyslexic student experiences this. However well you know your material it seems impossible to get it down on paper.

## If you are *dyslexic*

Ideas flash in and out of your mind.
You may put off the dreaded moment of actually starting to write by reading a lot.
You have lots of ideas all competing for your attention.
Ideas will just come tumbling out randomly.
No time to reorder your ideas, or you are unsure which ideas to develop.

## If you are *dyspraxic*

Writing can present several issues:

- Handwriting can be difficult physically to coordinate and lack legibility
- Sorting information and structuring assignments
- Formatting as required takes extra time and effort.

These issues may lead to comments such as:

> *Interesting points but lacks analysis.*

> *Lots of good ideas, but lacks structure.*

Unfortunately, a confused writer leads to a confused reader, and lower marks.

 **TOP TIP** Planning is essential to avoid confusing both yourself and your reader!

## Planning is positive and reduces your workload

Planning …

Gives you an overview

Sorts out your thoughts

Makes you look at different views

Eliminates unnecessary material

Shows up where you have lack of evidence

Identifies areas where you need to research and fill in gaps

Allows you to break the task down into manageable chunks

Fits into the dyslexic learning style

Keeps you on track …

Some very simple planning will save a lot of time and trouble. Ideally, your essay will go straight from the introduction, through a series of logical steps, to the conclusion:

Unfortunately, many students' assignments end up looking like this:

Planning helps avoid this result by breaking the task down into manageable chunks.

## First plan (pre-planning)

**Collect:** Blank computer page or paper (A3 if possible) and pencil, coloured pens or highlighters.

**OK, go! Write, anything ...** Spend a few minutes just getting down *any* ideas that occur to you. Bullet point ideas, mind map or just randomly write.

Don't worry about sorting ideas out for the moment, just get them down.

**Next:**

1 **Mark your work** with a ✓ (or Y for Yes if typing), X (or strike through ~~abc~~ if typing) or ?

    ✓   (Y if typing)    anything that you *must* include

    **X**   (~~abc~~ if typing)    anything that does not seem to fit in, or you can't find information (evidence) about

    ?                   anything you are not sure about or would like to include but may not have room for

2 **Colour code** anything you think goes together: just circle, strike through or highlight the word, or change the font colour if typing.

Each colour should represent one idea. You now have a basic plan of ideas you may develop.

This can be turned into your assignment! Later ideas can be added in a different colour.
   This is your first plan – see p. 96 for developing your plan.

# The shape of anything written!

Any well-written text has a diamond shape!

**Introduction**

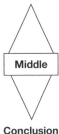

**Middle**

**Conclusion**

**Introduction:** Tells the reader why the subject is important and how the author will deal with it

**Middle:** Consists of a series of steps examining the subject

*leading to*

**Conclusion:** Discusses where it went and any implication of this

This applies to all kinds of writing: essays, reports, chapters in books and dissertations. Remembering this will improve the structure of whatever you are writing.

# Shape your assignment

Before doing any planning, 'shape' your assignment. First, make your work fit within any word count or page count. It is *much* easier to do this at the start than have to rewrite at the end to make it fit.

A bit of basic maths is all you need. For a 2,000-word assignment:

Introduction

Middle

Conclusion

**Introduction:** 10% of the word count; just knock the final zero off the total word count
**So: 2,000 = 200 words**

**Middle:** 80% = **1,600 words**

**Conclusion:** 10% of the word count
**So: 2,000 = 200 words**

### Dividing up the middle: 1,600 words

Look at your colour-coded pre-planning; each colour should be one theme to develop.

If you have 4 themes, divide the middle word count by 4.

> 1600/4 = 400 words for each section

You do not have to use exactly 400 words for each section; this is just a guide to start off with.

Word counts are useful: they tell you how much (or, even better, how little) research you need to do.

> The word count is your budget. Stick to it! It takes a lot of time to adjust this at the end if you have written too much

## Planning tools

With your word count in mind you can develop your plan. The planning tool you use to do this is your choice. Here are some suggestions:

Boxes                          Mindmapping

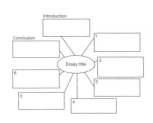
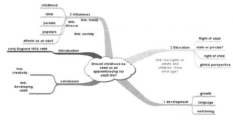

Example by Amanda (Early Childhood Studies)

PowerPoint slides

Table or matrix

| Point | Evidence | Example | So ... |
|-------|----------|---------|--------|
|       |          |         |        |
|       |          |         |        |

Post-it notes (the computer version is Stickies)

Or use anything else you think will work for you. Think back: is there something you did in the past that worked well for you? Don't think that now you are a university student this may not work for you anymore. You may have to adapt it, of course.

If you are working in a group you could do this online, with everyone contributing. Try Lucidchart.com for mind maps and flow diagrams, free for Google accounts.

*Lucy's friend helped her out when he made her a Word document with text boxes in it and told her she could only write about one thing in each box. Brilliantly simple – but this enabled Lucy to write perfect paragraphs.*

# Developing your plan

It is best to first FRAME and then FILL in your plan. Don't worry about having all the information needed to write the assignment. The gaps can be filled in later.

**Frame and fill** is when you have your first plan ( see pp. 90–91 ) and use this as an outline (or frame) for your assignment. This means you start with a series of headings to which you add later.

Arrabella's mind map can be turned into a framework for her essay:

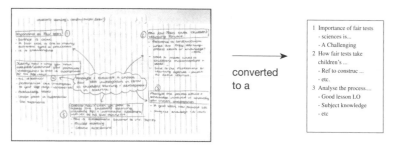

Mind map

converted to a

framework for her essay

Most mind mapping software or apps can also do this for you. You make a mind map and the software program can convert it to a linear outline (your frame!).

Carol (Foundation Ministry) used Inspiration software to produce her mind map and a linear framework for her to 'fill in'.

Each idea (represented on your plan by a mind map branch, Post-it note, PowerPoint slide, or box) now needs to be turned into a paragraph.

# What is where in the assignment?

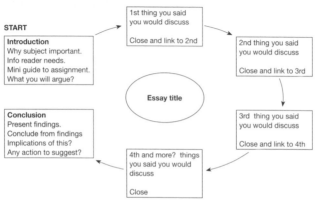

**START**

**Introduction**
Why subject important.
Info reader needs.
Mini guide to assignment.
What you will argue?

**Conclusion**
Present findings.
Conclude from findings
Implications of this?
Any action to suggest?

Essay title

1st thing you said
you would discuss

Close and link to 2nd

2nd thing you said
you would discuss

Close and link to 3rd

3rd thing you said
you would discuss

Close and link to 4th

4th and more? things
you said you would
discuss

Close

Notice that the introduction and conclusion are side by side. These should 'mirror' each other. Put these side by side when you write the conclusion so you can clearly see where everything you said you would do in the introduction went.

  Should mirror

## Avoid long paragraphs

Do the paragraph hand test: hold your hand up and spread your thumb and first finger out. Keep your paragraphs no longer than that! So, about two paragraphs per page.

(With thanks to Kate Williams, 2011)

## What should be in a paragraph?

Every paragraph should develop ONE point only. Each paragraph also follows the diamond structure.

> **Open:** Clearly indicate the idea to be discussed – what the paragraph is about, the point you will develop
>
> **Middle:** Provide supporting evidence for, and maybe against, your point
>
> **Close and link:** Where are you now? Can you show how this links to the question? Are there any implications? (This is where you show *your* voice in the paragraph)

## How long should a paragraph be?

Your poor reader cannot concentrate for a whole page of dense text (and neither can you!). Do the 'upside down test' to see if your paragraphs are too long. Print your work out (single-sided is best). Lay it out *upside down*. You should see clear blocks (one block = one paragraph which develops one point).

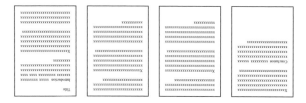

If it looks like this, the paragraphs need sorting out:

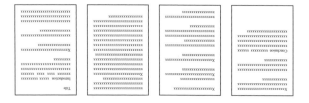

## Paragraph checker

**Use WEED** to check the paragraph is complete.

**W**hat: Is it clear what point you will develop?

**E**vidence: The main point must be supported (or questioned) using evidence from your reading and research. So, every paragraph should contain at least one reference and usually more.

**E**xample: Is an example needed? (Not always.)

**D**o: So what? What will you do with this now? Can you show how this links to the question?

**Paragraph planner/checker memory aid**

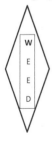

## Paragraph showing WEED

**W** = What

Transition is the inner movement or journey we make in reaction to a change.

**E** = Evidence

Lewin's (1951) model of change management describes the need to unfreeze, change and refreeze the organisation in order to continue with the change and prevent regression to the former systems.

**E** = Example (not always needed)

In order to help the junior members of the team, leaders were attempting to provide education and staff support; this has been difficult at times due to lack of staff and time. The team may have not become so disheartened and split if the Trust had acknowledged the need for financial investment to support the change. Hayes (2008 p. 179) states, "the key to modernisation is the need to change attitudes and culture within the health care service".

**D** = Do

Therefore leadership using the best strategies for the type of change may help influence staff to work towards the change.

(Julie, Healthcare)

# Critical thinking

Be aware:

▸ you need to **present an argument**: simply *describing* what you have found out gets *limited marks*

▸ most marks are for **analysing and evaluating evidence**

▸ you should draw **mini conclusions** throughout the assignment – the 'Do' at the end of the paragraph (see above) – and bring these forward to the overall conclusion.

To see how to move from being descriptive to being analytical and drawing conclusions, see the Critical Thinking model at: www.plymouth.ac.uk/uploads/production/document/path/1/1713/Model_To_Generate_Critical_Thinking.pdf and RMIT resources at: https://emedia.rmit.edu.au/learninglab/content/critical-thinking-basics.

At the **end of a paragraph**, it may help to:

▸ Check you are still *focusing on the idea* you started off with.

▸ Look back to the question: *have you developed and moved on the argument?*

▸ Consider what your *mini conclusion* is for this paragraph.

▸ Is the *mini conclusion* an important point? If so, add it to your *final conclusion*.

# Using assistive technology to help writing

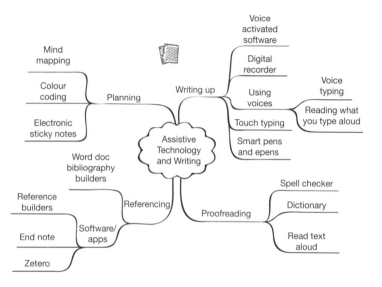

Mind mapping
Colour coding
Electronic sticky notes
Planning

Voice activated software
Digital recorder
Using voices
Touch typing
Smart pens and epens
Writing up

Voice typing
Reading what you type aloud

Assistive Technology and Writing

Word doc bibliography builders
Reference builders
End note
Zetero
Software/ apps
Referencing

Spell checker
Dictionary
Read text aloud
Proofreading

## Voice or touch typing – why it is a good idea

When you are writing, there is a lot going on. You are having to:

Recall    Reword    Rework information    AND    Remember it while you write it down

Being dyslexic makes remembering and processing information much harder than for non-dyslexics, and the act of writing adds in another process. This simply overloads everything so you lose track of what you were trying to say.

Voice or touch typing means one of these processes becomes automatic so you do not have to think about it consciously. This lightens the load, and students who can voice or touch type report that it helps significantly.

Use **speech-to-text software/apps** to voice type, find these:

touch typing

▸ On your PC, you may have to search for speech-to-text software or apps in preferences or settings; or use YouTube to find how to add the software or app to your toolbar
▸ Google Docs, voice typing: find it under tools
▸ Smartphones: use built-in or download dictation apps
▸ Dragon speaking software: if you have DSA funding, check if you have this.

It is well worth the effort of learning to touch or voice type. You can find free 'typing tutor' software online or from: www.dyslexic.com.

## Referencing is harder if you are dyslexic/dyspraxic

You find:

Sequencing information is affected by memory & processing speed

The author said it perfectly

I lack the confidence to change words

It's really hard to recall where you found info

Over learning means you recall whole lines of text

TOP TIP Referencing needs extra care and generally takes longer than you expect it to

## Referencing: using your computer

Try these:

Use **Word References** tab to build your bibliography. Most referencing styles covered.

Your uni may subscribe to **referencing software** such as *Cite them right online* or EndNote; find out and get help to use them. Zotero is a free online alternative.

**Colour code** sections of your work for different sources. *All information from book by Smith in red. Article by Jones in blue.* Make sure you note colour used for different sources!

Create your own **mini referencing guide**. Copy and paste from online uni guides or you can email examples using the app or software. Copy examples into your work so you can follow the correct style. Remember to delete the example!

Start your mini guide with:
- Book
- Journal
- Journal accessed from a database
- Web articles

Add other examples as you use them.

Use **online reference builders or apps**. Any references collected this way must be carefully checked against your uni's referencing guidelines. Take care not to mix and match styles: consistency of style is important.

**TOP TIP** Add in your references as you go. Save yourself from a horrible job at the end!

## Colour coding references

You could colour code your referencing guide if you think it would help sequence the information.

Author (date) title edition? Place: Publisher

Godwin J (2014) *Planning your essay* (2nd edn). London: Palgrave.

> Use your smartphone to photograph or scan the book cover or title pages so you have all the information needed for the reference. Some apps, for example Cite This For Me, allow you to scan the barcode and send the reference to yourself. Do check it fits with your uni's style of referencing though.

## Plagiarism

Plagiarism is when you use someone else's work (or idea) in your assignment and don't make it clear where you got it from. This means you are presenting it as your idea, even if you didn't mean to.

Avoiding plagiarism is easy once you understand when you have to reference.

# How do I know what should be referenced and what shouldn't?

Ask yourself:

| Question | Comment | Do I have to reference it? |
|----------|---------|---------------------------|
| Did you have to read it to know it? | Where did you find it? If you read it somewhere, you should reference it. | Yes |
| Is it your own idea? | If your idea has developed from the evidence you have already referenced, you don't need to reference it again. This is your idea. | No. Your reader can see that you have progressed from the (referenced) research. Worth extra marks as this puts 'your voice' into your work. |
| Is it your own idea? | Are you sure you didn't find it out somewhere? | Probably. Unless you are asked to present your original ideas, it is best to avoid this. |
| Does everybody know it? | No need to reference it then. | No |
| Is it common knowledge in your subject area? | No need to reference it; it may be hard to find out whose idea it originally was. | No, but if in doubt reference it. |
| How do I know this? | You didn't just wake up knowing this! | Probably |

## How do I know what should be referenced and what shouldn't? (cont.)

| Question | Comment | Do I have to reference it? |
|---|---|---|
| Did you put someone's idea into your own words? | It is still their idea. | Yes |
| Did you quote directly? | You must also include the page number. | Yes (include page number or put 'no page' if this is not given). |

 **TOP TIP** The golden rule is: if in doubt, reference it.

## Avoiding plagiarism

Follow this good practice and you will avoid plagiarism:

▶ Allow plenty of time to do your work – it is tempting to copy if you are rushing.
▶ Make a note of where you find information.
▶ When taking notes, record the full reference at the top of the page.
▶ When paraphrasing, try not to look back at the original until you have written it in your own words; then check it is correct against the original.

For more on referencing, see *Referencing and Understanding Plagiarism* in this series.

# Paraphrasing: putting it in YOUR own words

You can use exactly the same words as the author if you reference it as a direct quote: **'if you do this you must reference it correctly AND add the page number'** (Godwin 2017 p. xx).

Quoting, however, only shows your reader you found it, not that you understood it. So you always need to explain a quote. When you put it into your own words, you demonstrate you truly 'got it'.

Or you can put it into your own words by paraphrasing. Of course, this is not always easy – you may like the way the writer put it and feel they said it perfectly.

Paraphrasing should **summarise** information and **show you understood it**. You **MUST** still reference when you paraphrase. It is still the author's idea even though you used your own words.

**Try this technique:**
- Read the passage – try to work out the main idea.
- Write down 4 or 5 main words from it on a separate piece of paper. Can you change any of them? If so, cross out the original one and use the new one.
- Leave it for a few minutes.
- Try to write it in your own words, or you could record this or use voice typing.

> Check the main idea is the same – if not, repeat the process.
> Check you have not used exactly the same words.

Summarising by paraphrasing is hard, but the benefit is you really learn your stuff; this will show in your work and grades.

 **TOP TIP** Don't forget: you still need to reference whenever you paraphrase.

For more on referencing see *Referencing and Understanding Plagiarism* in this series.

## Proofreading tips

Let's be honest, proofreading is never going to be a strong point of yours. But there are times you cannot avoid this. These tips will help with the main issues:

▸ **Write short sentences**: one idea, one sentence. Check your work for any sentences that are 4 lines or more long. Are there two ideas here? If so, split them up into 2 sentences.

▸ **Read it out loud**: you will often be able to hear mistakes you cannot see. Use assistive technology text-to-speech (TTS) software to do this for you. Try Google Chrome extension Speak It, ClaroSpeak, or NaturalReader.

▸ **Spelling**: try to pick the right one, of course, but then be consistent. Your reader will forgive an error, but swapping between versions will just get on their nerves. Use assistive technology to help (see below).

 Get someone whose English you trust
to read it over for you!

# Spelling: why it is an issue and how you can cope with this

Spelling will usually be a problem if you are dyslexic. This is because your memory and processing difficulties interfered with your ability to process phonological information when you were learning to read, and may still do so. It means your spelling can be erratic and vary from day to day. When you are stressed or working to a deadline your spelling may be much worse than usual.

**Some students find these helpful:**

▶ **Computer spell checker:** If you get a red wiggly line under a word, then check it. Right clicking should come up with suggestions to start with. A green wiggly line is a grammatical error. Unless it changes your meaning, go with it; it is usually correct.

▶ **Assistive technology:** Spell checkers and dictionaries in assistive technology programs are much better than ordinary spell checkers for Word documents. So run your work through these before handing it in. They also build up knowledge of the correct spellings for the words you use most often and will autocorrect words. These include:

  ▶ If you have DSA funding, you may get Texthelp, ClaroRead or Global AutoCorrect

  ▶ If you do not have funding, try Ginger Spell Checker or Hemingway Editor. Hemingway Editor colour codes where your writing is hard to follow. Helpfully, it tells you why this is so, so you can correct it.

- **Keep a spelling book:** Circle spellings in your work you suspect are wrong. When you have found the correct spellings enter them in your spelling book. (An address book is good for this.) Add a brief explanation or you will be looking it up again. Beware of false friends, though – a word with different meanings may have a different spelling. Example: to, too and two. Keeping a spelling book does not suit everyone, so only do this if it helps.
- **Online dictionaries:** You can try online dictionaries such as dictionary.com. Beware using the thesaurus, though, if you are at all unsure of the meaning. You may be saying something very different to what you meant! Specialist online dictionaries can be very useful so try to locate one for your subject.
- **Ebooks**: These may have a facility to check the meaning of words.

You will be expected to be able to use and to spell the terminology associated with your subject and you will need to make an extra special effort to do this.

## Use MUSP to learn your spellings

Everyone has spellings they find difficult. At university you are coming across new words every day. You cannot learn all the new spellings at once, but if you tackle 4–6 a week using Jenny Lee's MUSP system: http://cw.routledge.com/textbooks/9780415597562/spelling5.asp, you will soon build up a bank of words you commonly use that you can spell.

**MUSP** stands for **M**ulti-**S**ensory **S**pelling **P**rogramme. MUSP uses overlearning and a range of techniques – visual, auditory and kinaesthetic – which fit in with your dyslexic and individual learning style.

Try to review and practise 4–6 spellings a week. Continue reviewing spellings for about a month, then review at intervals to make sure you can still recall the spelling. If you start to misspell the word again, just add it to the weekly list.

Pick a word you misspell and try the MUSP method.

## The MUSP method explained

| What to do | An example |
|---|---|
| **Pick a word you know you misspell:** write it out a few times. It doesn't matter if you misspell it several ways | elephent elephaint<br>elephant elefant |
| **Find the correct spelling**: use a dictionary, textbook or spell checker | elephant |
| **Identify where the error occurs**: underline this, notice the correct way | eleph<u>ent</u> |

| | |
|---|---|
| **Choose a strategy**: to help you remember the correct way to spell the word. You can be creative here | an elephant stepping on an ant |
| **LOOK** at the word and strategy | |
| **SAY** the word and strategy | |
| **COVER** the word and strategy | |
| **SAY** the word and strategy, **PICTURE** each part in your mind | |
| **SAY** the strategy as you **WRITE** the word | *'The elephant steps on the ant'* |
| **CHECK** | |
| *Source:* Adapted from Jenny Lee's (2000) MUSP Spelling Programme for Priority Words. | |

Repeat this process with different words until you have a short list – no more than 10 new words a week. Practise your list daily using the MUSP technique. Drop words from the list once you are confident you can spell them correctly.

## Memory (and forgetting)

Everyone forgets what they have learnt if they don't review it later on.

The good news is that once you have learnt it thoroughly it stays with you in your long-term memory. The trick is learning it well enough for this to happen.

This graph represents how much is forgotten without reviewing (80%) and how much remembered when reviewed (100%). This is why the Cornell note-taking system works – it builds in regular reviewing (see pp. 47–49).

*The forgetting (and remembering) curve*

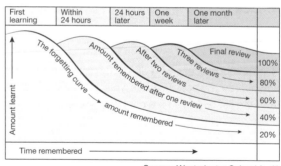

*Source:* Westminster School (n.d.)

In dyslexia/SpLD this process is slower and not as sure because your short-term memory and slower speed of processing mean everything takes much longer.

So you need to start earlier – and be clever about how you tackle your revision to suit your dyslexic learning style. Review the pages on short-term memory and dyslexia learning style to remind you why doing LITTLE and OFTEN helps (see p. 12).

## Tackling revision in a dyslexia/SpLD-friendly way

There are three things to consider here:
1 Reduce the amount tackled.
2 Apply the LITTLE and OFTEN strategy to revision.
3 Use your individual learning style: visual, hearing, active (or a bit of each!).

### Reducing the amount tackled

At first it may seem you know nothing and have it all to do. But you have been to lectures and tackled some of the reading so you *do* know something already.

Now you need to target your revision – tackling everything is impossible:
1 Only learn off by heart essential information such as names, dates and formulas. Then concentrate on understanding the main concepts or ideas so you can demonstrate your understanding.

**2** Look through your course information – it may help to do a mind map of what was covered each week. Have a look at past papers quickly if you have them. Which topics are more likely to come up? Did you have any clues from tutors? Target these first.

**3** Make a note of any gaps in your notes you need to fill. Do these as soon as you can. Then have a go at planning answers to any questions you have (past papers or mock exams) or make up your own questions.

Set yourself clear targets – a 'to do' list is useful for this and will help you monitor your progress. Sometimes you have to make a 'strategic decision' to miss a topic out due to lack of time.

> *Amber (a foundation Science student) knew there was no way she could get her head round the genetics topic in time for the exam, so she abandoned it and revised her 3 other topics better – a calculated risk that paid off.*

## Applying LITTLE and OFTEN

In the panic of revision it is easy to forget to use the LITTLE and OFTEN learning style which helps deal with the dyslexic issues of memory and overlearning. Try to work out how long you can work efficiently for different activities and stick to this:

- Most importantly, STOP or switch activity when you notice your attention is drifting.
- Work out when you work best – and save tough topics for then (see p. 28).

If you are dyspraxic, you may be able to study for longer periods but even so you are unlikely to be taking in information after 40 minutes or so.

### Taking mini breaks is *vital* if you are dyslexic

If you are dyslexic, you need to take lots of breaks so you don't overload too much. Even when you are not working your brain is still trying to make sense of things. Do you sometimes wake up with a solution to a problem? Your hardworking brain was hard at it while you slept! Be confident: mini breaks mean more is learnt in the end.

**Keeping going ...** Have lots of mini treats lined up (and some bigger ones for time off).

| Mini treat | Chocolate bar or luxury coffee, a 10-minute walk, the gym, a phone call, 10 mins on social media, cook a favourite meal<br>Your suggestions? |
| Bigger treat | The cinema, a long walk, a meal out<br>Your suggestions? |

**Try not to revise up to the last minute**

*Joe, doing Law, always took the night off before an exam. He went to a concert, play or film and was still fresh for the exam. Joe said working till the last minute didn't give enough time 'for it to sink in'.*

**When should I start?**

Start as soon as you can! If you get into the habit of constantly reviewing work, revision will be much easier to deal with. So if you know you have an exam, try to follow this:

| Same day as lectures | Review notes later the same day or ASAP. Use Cornell (see pp. 47–49) or summarise on a sticky note or Post-it note |
| Within a week | Review summary, note in review column/margin any missing info or questions you have – use a different colour so you can spot additions easily |

| Within 3 weeks | If it is a likely exam topic: follow up any missing notes and find past papers – are there any questions on this topic? If so, start some active revision – whatever you like: cards, mind map, recording or talking aloud |
|---|---|
| Until you start seriously revising | Continue reviewing everything – at least glance through it weekly and more often if possible. Even brief reviewing will help |

### Revision timetables: to do or not to do?

A too strict revision timetable can be unhelpful. It is a bit like following a diet: if you slip up and fail to hit your target you get fed up with yourself and may give up.

Try to make any timetable realistic. A mini slip-up is OK, it is human! Just keep going. Dyslexia/SpLD means it takes longer to do things, *not* that you can't do it.

If a revision timetable has helped before, do this, but include lots of mini breaks. Brain. HE (2006) has a downloadable revision planner and excellent revision strategies at: www.brainhe.com/students/types/ExamsandRevision.html.

| Time | Mon | Tue | Wed | Thurs | Fri | Sat | Sun |
|---|---|---|---|---|---|---|---|
| 9 | | Make list Soc topics | Psychol wk 7-9 | | | Practice paper | |
| 10 | Gym | Select topics, find notes | | Library - get past papers | Gym | | |
| 11 | | Look up SD | Meet group | | | | |
| 12 | Stats, find notes | Lunch | Plan essay | Stats 2 topics review | Review notes | | |
| 1 | Walk | Mock | Lunch Emma | | | | |
| 2 | Psychol Wk 1-3 notes review | Mock | Mind map Soc module | Café - Joe | | Travel | |
| 3 | | Mock | Find Soc books | Practise Paper 2 notes | | | |
| 4 | Call home | Coffee | Walk | | | Football | |
| 5 | Cook | Psychol Wk 4-6 | Notes for Q3 | Swim | | Football | |
| 6 | 'To do' list for week | Write Q | Cook | Stat Chap 2 | | Travel | |
| 7 | Stats notes find gaps | Shop | Select 3 topics, find exam Q | Film night | | Review past paper | |
| 8 | | Cook | Plan 1 Q | | | | |
| 9 | | Topics for 2mw | Drink with Dan | | | | |

But if this seems too regimented, a simple list, as below, may work just as well.

| Time | Activity |
|---|---|
| 20 mins | Collect notes on ... |
| 20 mins | Write out possible questions for ... |
| 10 mins | Tidy up room |
| 20 mins | Plan brief answer for 1 question |
| 20 mins | Check against notes/textbook, highlight problem bits |
| 20 mins | Break |

Don't spend hours on this – it is a tool and does not have to look pretty!

## Using what works best for your learning style

You can use any of these:

- visual – by seeing
- auditory – by hearing/listening
- kinaesthetic – by doing (action or movement)
- or a mixture of all of them – try whatever works for you.

**Amount recalled when reading, listening, seeing, speaking and doing**

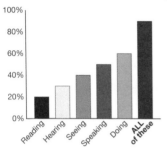

*Source:* Flanagan 1997, cited in Cottrell 2008 p. 308.

So mixing and matching these activities is a good idea!

Don't dismiss what has worked for you in the past – just adapt it.

*Joe, a Law student, used different coloured cards (and shapes) to distinguish between criminal law and tort in order to learn 200+ cases. Despite his very slow processing, Joe was the only student on the course to do this and he got a First.*

The message here is be inventive about revision: ***don't just read.*** Be ACTIVE in your revision!

# Revising actively: what could you use?

**Ways to revise 'actively'**

### Visual (seeing)

- Mind maps, brainstorming, sketches, diagrams.
- Display on walls.
- Coloured pens, shapes, cards.
- Mnemonics – first letters of words to make a word to aid recall (e.g. SQ3R for **S**urvey, **Q**uestion, **R**ead, **R**ecall **R**eview).
- Post-it notes.
- Textmapping (see p. 83).
- Evernote, Google Keep, erasable white board, books, roll of self-adhesive, whiteboard paper, use smartphones to take photos and scans.

### Auditory (hearing)

- Record questions and, later on, answers.
- Record information.
- Use audio notetaker (p. 46).
- Question yourself as if you were interviewing.
- Use assistive technology to read out loud.
- 'Study buddy' or group revision.
- Smartpens, dictation apps, Google voice typing.

### Kinaesthetic (doing)

- Walk or move while revising (exercise bike?).
- Act out scenarios.
- Use a stress ball, or bounce a ball while recalling information.
- Imagine a walk or rooms in a house – attach information to objects. Recall objects/ information as you imagine the walk.
- Large mind maps (or textmapping, see p. 83) on the floor.
- Do past papers.
- Walk around every 20–30 mins.
- Flashcards – try Quizlet or StudyBlue revision apps.

You can of course use a mixture of these – but do use some of them.

# Dealing with distractions: what will be your strategy?

Don't worry about short distractions – 10 minutes or so – these are helpful for your dyslexic/SpLD learning style. But if you are taking more breaks than working, consider how to change this.

Distractions will happen sometimes! What are your most common distractions?

- Social media
- ?
- ?

If you are constantly on the internet and social media, use this as a reward after a period of study: 1 hour study time = 10 mins online.

Some websites/apps can monitor how you spend your time – this may be a revelation! Use self-control apps to block sites and help you keep focused on your studies.

Think ahead how to deal with distractions: *'I can meet for coffee, but not a night out this week.'*

Or, like Abdullah, make it work for YOU!

*Abdullah realised he was doing a lot of his friend's revision for him by chatting on social media. He made this work for him by only discussing areas he needed to cover, so getting his own work done at the same time.*

## Be kind to yourself

Exams are stressful, so make sure you eat and sleep as well as you can. Being tired or feeling sluggish because of a bad diet won't help.

Stress is normal and, under control, even helpful. Keeping as stress-free as possible will reduce the impact of dyslexia/SpLD.

## If it is all getting out of hand

Do contact your university support service if you are overstressed or dealing with your stress in an unhelpful way, such as avoiding work or using alcohol or drugs.

Your mental and physical health comes first. Don't be scared to seek help if you need to. Check online to see what help is available at your uni or college. You could try apps such as MindShift or Headspace.

 Exams are important – but it is not the end of the world if you fail one

## The night before an exam

| What to do | Check you have |
|---|---|
| *Set your alarm* | At least one, and the sound is on! |
| *Pack* | What you need: pen, ruler, calculator etc. |
| *Check details* | Time. Place. How long for? |
| *Check exam format if you can* | Worked out possible times per question |
| *Eat* | Eaten properly! Something to eat for breakfast? |
| *Know what time to leave home* | Added enough time for it to go wrong! |
| *Know how to travel there* | Checked any timetables and have enough money for fares |
| *Sleep* | Set the alarm |

 TOP TIP Try to relax, get as much sleep as possible.
Avoid last-minute revision

## Why do I find exams so difficult?

The combination of these 'ingredients' in the exam makes it hard for you to produce accurate, clearly structured answers within the time allowed.

Many dyslexic/SpLD students try to choose units of study that are *not* assessed by exam, or where the exam is only part of the assessment. Avoiding exams is not always possible, however, as many courses have in-class tests or practical-based assessments.

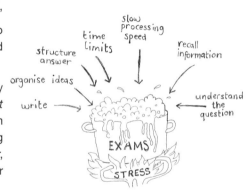

You should be entitled to 25% extra time if you have had a full post-16 dyslexia assessment, which details any extra support provisions available to you.

# Extra time and other exam provisions

Most dyslexic/SpLD students get 25% extra time allowed for exams.

**25% = 15 minutes extra time for each hour of the exam.**

This is to compensate for the longer time it takes you to process the written information on the exam paper and recall, sequence and write down your answer.

You may also be allocated an exam room with other SpLD students. This may be a smaller room with less noise and distractions than large exam halls.

Depending on what is recommended in your assessment (see p. 158), you may also be allowed to use a computer or even a scribe in the exam. Consider carefully how you will use these in an exam and remember Word checker facilities or access to online resources will not be allowed.

Research shows stress increases the effect of dyslexia. This includes crunch times such as coursework deadlines or exams.

Learn to use your extra time constructively, gain marks and be less stressed in the exam.

# Thinking back over past exam performance

This will be helpful to improve your future exam performance. So be honest!

Tick any of the following you know have happened to you.

| What happened? | ✓ or ✗ | See page |
|---|---|---|
| Ran out of time | | p. 134 |
| Wrote down everything I could think of | | p. 135 |
| Gave short answer then got stuck | | pp. 135–136 |
| Missed out part of the question | | p. 136 |

These are costing you marks, so read on.

Other problems are:

▶ answering the wrong number of questions

▶ wrongly numbering questions on the answer paper.

*These are typical errors so double- and triple-check for these.*

## Running out of time

Time management in the exam is vital – usually it takes longer than you thought to answer questions. See also *Time Management* in this series.

*Strictly* work out how much time you have for each question and stick to this

You always pick up more marks if you attempt ALL the required questions. Most marks are gained at the start of your answer and tail off as you start to repeat or include irrelevant information.

## Writing down everything you know about a subject

You just start to write down everything you can recall about that subject. This is caused by a lack of confidence in what the question actually means. Time spent analysing the question will be well spent (pp. 139–140).

## Giving too short answers: your answers are not detailed enough

The problem here is not developing an answer – answering the question but not providing supporting evidence. The examiner wants you to show the thinking behind your answer. This usually means doing some critical analysis.

**Try these ways to develop your answer:**

- Useful questions such as the 5 Ws: **W**hat, **W**hy, **W**hen, **W**here and **W**ho (and **H**ow!).
- Ask yourself why the examiner asked the question. Usually, it is so you can show your knowledge and understanding **and** apply this to an imaginary scenario.

## Missing out part of the question

Two-part (or more) questions are tricky. It is easy to start answering the first part of the question, which may seem quite simple, then forget to do the other parts.

**Example:**

*Outline the key issues … Select one key issue you have discussed and …*

*1st part: Outline … show you know the main ideas*

*2nd part: analytical, focuses on 1 or 2 issues in depth*

**So:**

1st part of question

2nd part of question

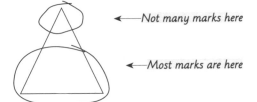

←— Not many marks here

←— Most marks are here

This is because you get more marks for **analysing** and **evaluating** the evidence rather than just describing it.

Ask yourself **critical questions**, such as:

▶ HOW does this work?
▶ WHY is it like that?

You can come to a **judgement** or **evaluation** about it.

Take more time on the second part of the question where the marks are

## Answering the wrong number of questions

It happens! Check and double-check.

*In her law exam Fatima answered all 8 questions, when she was asked to only do 3. It was a 2-hour exam (so she had 2 ½ hours with her extra time). Despite all her efforts she failed. Obviously she could not give enough detail in 15–20 minutes per question when she should really have allowed herself 40–50 minutes for each one.*

## A note about proofreading

If you really think proofreading will get you extra marks, leave 10 minutes at the end for this. BUT, for most dyslexics, proofreading does not work, so in an exam don't bother.

**Do check your work** for errors in science, maths and multiple choice questions.

# Using your extra time constructively

The extra time is useful, because it:

▶ reduces stress
▶ allows time to plan or structure your answer.

Avoid making the same old errors by first checking you know how to tackle any problem areas you have (see p. 133). Next, consider how to use your extra time more constructively in future.

Give yourself permission to use the extra time to:

▶ work out your timings in the exam
▶ analyse the question
▶ plan your answer.

These are real time savers, so don't be tempted just to start writing. It will cost you more time in the end.

 **TOP TIP** Work out your timings in the exam

Carefully check you have selected the right number of questions, and decide which order to do them in.

# Analysing the question

**Helpful types of words** in the question are given below.

| Word type | Example | Function |
|---|---|---|
| Process (sometimes called the instruction, direction or keyword) | Discuss, evaluate, critically analyse, briefly outline | Tells you the process you have to do; also indicates depth of research required |
| Subject or content | The main area under discussion | Broad focus of answer; try to stick to this only |
| Limit or scope | Dates, geographical area, number of examples | Focuses the area to be examined; note this carefully |
| Other **significant** words – key aspects | Any other aspects not covered above | Pinpointing the limit or scope of answer |

*Source:* Adapted from Williams (1995).

Use highlighters to identify the different types of words in the question:

Compare and contrast the role and powers of the House of Representatives and the Senate.

Process or instruction words

Limit or scope of the question: stick to this!

The subject or content

## Planning your answer in the exam

You can use any planning methods you feel happy with: mind map, bullet points, table/matrix (see pp. 94–95 for more). Decide if you want to plan all the answers first, or one by one as you tackle them.

For each question:
1 Take a few minutes to write down everything you can think of.
2 Now reread the question and add ✓ ✗ ?.
3 Now number all the ticks in the order you think best.

Do any of the ? bits seem to fit in? Unless you are sure, forget them for now. When you are writing you may see where they fit in.

**This is your mini plan. Now you can start!**

If it is an essay, write:

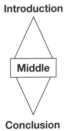

Introduction

Middle

Conclusion

**Brief introduction:** Say why it is important and the main areas you will cover: refer to your plan!

**The middle:** Write at least one paragraph for each point on your plan. Look back at the question at the end of each paragraph. Can you point out how it addressed the question?

**The conclusion:** Briefly say what the main points were. Why is this important?

## What to do if you go blank

This happens to everyone sometimes. Try these:

▶ leave a space, it may come back later
▶ relax – try tensing *all* your muscles and then, starting at the head, relax them one by one
▶ go back to the title, pick out keywords, scribble notes on anything you can remember about these for 2 minutes.

In extreme circumstances, take a mental break. Think of a time or place when you felt happy. Relive the moment in your head for a minute or two to calm you down. If you 'blank' often, choose this time/place in advance for a quick getaway.

## After the exam

**Now,** forget it. There is no more you can do and worrying will only stress you.

**Later on,** before the next exam, think about what happened. See p. 133 for possible problems and suggestions.

### What happened?

| Before the exam | During | After | Action |
|---|---|---|---|
| Preparation good | Planning awful | Remembered something I missed out | Practise planning! See pp. 89–97 |
| - | Froze | - | Think about how I can deal with this next time. See p. 133 |
| Your thoughts here | | | |
| | | | |
| | | | |

# Multiple choice questions (MCQs)

MCQs test your dyslexia/SpLD as much as your subject knowledge. You need to process lots of similar information and recall matching information from your memory, all under timed conditions. This is a bit like a 'spot the difference' competition.

Obviously revising well will help you spot a matching answer quickly (once you have processed the question), making your response as automatic as possible.

After reading the question, **try to recall the answer before running through the options**. This reduces the amount of processing you do and makes the right answer easier to spot.

GUESS any questions you don't know; even if the exam is negatively marked this should pay off. If there are 4 possible answers and you can eliminate one and another looks unlikely, you have a 50% chance of being correct – and that is a pass.

## Seen exams

These are when you are told the questions beforehand so that you can research the answer. Alternatively, you may be given information; for example, a case study to learn/analyse before an exam. You will be told if you are allowed to take these or some brief notes into the exam.

| Do | Don't | Why |
|---|---|---|
| Make an outline plan ⇩ Make notes, write an answer from these ⇩ Try to write your answer without notes ⇩ Write the answer under exam conditions | Memorise an answer | You need to show your critical thinking skills |
| | Work out an answer with friends | Your work needs to be individual: you don't want to risk a plagiarism charge |

# Open book exams

| Issue | Solution |
|-------|----------|
| Searching and processing information is time-consuming | Practise finding out where information is in the book(s). Do this repeatedly until you have a visual map of it in your head |
| In the exam, don't look up everything | Revise the basic information so it is only the detail that needs to be looked up |
| If allowed to take an information sheet in, try not to just copy out chunks of info Try using Evernote or Google Keep to add pictures, scans etc. | It will be your analysis that carries marks Producing this will help you memorise information and make it interactive |

## Seminars: useful – and challenging!

Some dyslexic/SpLD students can excel in seminars, especially if they have a verbal/listening learning style. Seminars can be very constructive as they revisit the lecture, usually applying it to a real-life situation. Practising, discussing or doing a presentation on a scenario makes the purpose of what you are learning clearer.

Excellent though seminars can be, they can present issues for dyslexic/SpLD students:

▸ Seminars held shortly after the lecture do not allow time to review any lecture material before you have to apply this knowledge.
▸ Even when you know the answer to a question, it takes time to recall the answer or consider how to make a point. By the time you are ready, the moment has passed.
▸ Doing presentations is often a dyslexic/SpLD strength – but it needs good organisational (and sequencing) skills.

 When answering questions or making a point, keep sentences short and don't be tempted to overexplain

# Groupwork: making it work for you

Many dyslexic/SpLD students really enjoy groupwork. It allows them to do well at some aspects such as speaking and discussion without the need to read and write.

If you are a good talker, other students may just assume you are good at everything else. So be aware there are some pitfalls of groupwork for dyslexic/SpLD students.

| Beware! | Why? Because | Try this instead |
|---|---|---|
| Volunteering to do writing | You may be better at other stuff! | Making visual aids, presenting, advising? |
| Being unrealistic | It is hard to know how much you can do in a short time or within your timescale | 'Buddy up' to share tasks; take on less than you think you can manage! |
| Organisation issues | Times, dates and meetings are not your strong point | Note times/dates carefully. Make sure you have a reminder: online calendar, email, text, alarm |
| Overstimulation | If many ideas are suggested, you may get distracted or confused | Better to focus on one or two ideas only. Leave the rest to someone else |

**Most of all, enjoy it!**

 **STUDYING WITH DYSLEXIA**

# Keep a record of meetings

The record needs to include:

▸ who was present
▸ what was discussed
▸ any outcomes
▸ who will do what
▸ and by when.

This can be shared with the whole group in the 'cloud', for example in Google Drive. Do be aware, though, sharing folders shares ALL the content within that folder.

Groupwork   Record of meetings

Meeting no. ____   Date / time _____   Place _____

Group's research topic area
_____

Who present
_____
_____
_____

Outcomes of discussion
•
•
•

Actions

| WHAT needs doing? | WHO will do it? | HOW? Detail | By WHEN? |
|---|---|---|---|
|  |  |  |  |
|  |  |  |  |
|  |  |  |  |

Date and time of next meeting
_____

## Useful tools for groupwork

Online tools can be very useful:

- Arranging meetings:
  - The Doodle app is simple to use: http://doodle.com
  - Google Hangouts or Skype for when meetings are hard to arrange
- Sharing information:
  - Google Drive or other cloud-based storage
  - Trello
  - WhatsApp
  - Evernote (with other Evernote users).

Further useful information on groupwork can be found on the RMIT website: https://emedia.rmit.edu.au/learninglab/content/groupwork.

# Presentations

'Winging it' can be disastrous, as your dodgy short-term memory means you may:

▶ lose your place in the presentation
▶ get distracted and go off at a tangent
▶ skip bits you meant to include
▶ find it difficult to sequence your stuff
▶ find managing time problematic.

Even when you know your material well you need to do some planning to reduce the effect of your dyslexia/SpLD, which is always worse when you are under pressure.

### So, PLAN your presentation!

Plan:

▶ how you will keep on track
▶ what you will use to time it
▶ how you will start and end
▶ how you will deal with questions.

# Keeping on track

It doesn't matter what you use, but do use something – don't leave it to chance.

Cards

> **TOP TIP** Do NOT use lengthy notes – you may just end up reading them out!

# Managing time

- Avoid fiddling with your phone; set your timer going (check it is on silent).
- Write the finish time on top of your presentation notes/cards.
- Ask a friend to signal when you have just a few minutes left.
- Identify a chunk of material you can skim over (or miss out) if time is tight.

## Managing questions

Dealing with questions is best left to the end if you can, or you may go off track.

| Do | Why (and what to do if it goes wrong) |
|---|---|
| Repeat the question | To check you got it and so the audience knows what was asked |
| Answer the question | If you don't know, say: 'What an interesting point; does anyone know the answer to that?' If no one does (that will make you feel better!), say you will find out and ask the questioner to leave their details afterwards so you can get back to them (and do!) |
| Ask the questioner if that answered their question | To check if they are happy! If not, ask them to explain and start the process again |

PowerPoint is not the only presentation method; you could try Prezi. Online browser based Prezi allows you to zoom in and out of selected areas, add sound, animations, links and share this with up to 10 collaborators. There are also apps that allow you to make videos and voiceovers, such as 123-apps.

# 14 A final word: have confidence to study your own way!

The message from this book has been to think about how you learn best (metacognition) in order to improve your effectiveness. The strategies outlined can help but have the confidence to develop strategies of your own. If you are dyslexic use the LITTLE and OFTEN dyslexic learning style and do it *your* way.

If you have dyspraxia or another SpLD, do find out more about it and what techniques and strategies may be helpful for you. Start with the Useful contacts (p. 163) and Useful resources (p. 166) at the end of this book, but remember these are just start points. Do your own research as well.

## Be an ambassador for your SpLD and teach your tutors how to teach you!

- Ask for notes to be put on the VLE before lectures: explain that it helps you deal with the lecture content if you can preview notes.
- Ask if you can record what is said at meetings, including dissertation supervision meetings, or ask them to make notes for you: explain that it is not possible for you to listen and take notes simultaneously due to memory and processing difficulties.

Your tutors want to learn how best to support you, so it is up to you to (gently) guide them. Other dyslexic/SpLD students will benefit from this too.

## Support at university

There is excellent support at university for students with dyslexia or another SpLD. If you have funding from the DSA (Disabled Students' Allowance), you will not have to pay for this.

**This could provide access to:**

- one-to-one study skills support
- a computer with assistive software, and maybe a printer, scanner and digital recorder
- training to use the assistive software
- maybe an allowance for consumables such as paper, books, photocopying.

You can find out information about the DSA from DSA-QAG or www.yourdsa.com. See Useful contacts at the end of this book.

## Finding out what is available at your institution

Every university has a dyslexia/SpLD (specific learning difference) disability support team, usually situated within Student Services or Wellbeing. Universities vary in the way they organise support, so investigate what is available at your institution.

International, EU, part-time and some other students may not be eligible for DSA to fund their support. But your university may provide help you can access, so do ask!

For students without access to funding, there is an ever increasing amount of software and apps available that may help. Start with finding the latest available assistive technology advised by the excellent DnA Matters resources at: www.dnamatters.co.uk/resources.

## I think I may be dyslexic or have another SpLD: what next?

Dyslexia/SpLD does not just happen. If you are dyslexic or have another SpLD, you will always have had it. You may have learnt strategies to cope with it but it won't go away. It is worth investigating now.

There are free adult screeners or checklists available online, such as the one from the British Dyslexia Association: www.bdadyslexia.org.uk/screening. This has 15 questions. If your score indicates dyslexia is a possibility, contact your uni's dyslexia/

SpLD team. They can arrange for you to see a specialist to talk it over with. If they agree an SpLD is a possibility, they will recommend you have a full dyslexia/SpLD assessment and tell you how to arrange this.

For SpLDs other than dyslexia, refer to the Useful contacts page at the end of this book. Individual organisations for other SpLDs should be able to direct you to suitable checklists and advice.

## Why is an assessment needed?

A full diagnostic assessment is key to getting support for any SpLD or disability at university. This has to comply with guidelines and is required before you can apply for any funding, such as DSA. You cannot register at your university as a student requiring any kind of specialist support without this evidence.

## If I have had exam arrangements before, can I have them at uni?

Maybe! But if you had a short version of an assessment (usually called 'access arrangements') to allow extra time in exams or some extra support at college or school, this **MAY NOT be enough evidence** to register for support and apply for DSA at university.

Check with your uni's SpLD advisers. They will advise if you need to go for a full assessment and tell you how to do this if so.

## What happens at the assessment?

A full diagnostic assessment will take at least two hours and the final report may be many pages. It needs to test for the main characteristics of dyslexia or the SpLD for which you are being assessed; for dyslexia, these are difficulties with short-term memory, working memory and processing speed. Other tests may be done if you show signs of another SpLD, such as dyspraxia, ADHD or dyscalculia.

Some of the tests are quite fun and many students enjoy the activities, but of course there will be some tests you will find difficult if you have an SpLD. You cannot pass a SpLD assessment without revealing some underlying problems.

The assessor will ask some questions about your background and educational experience. The tests consider cognitive abilities, strengths and difficulties and come to a conclusion about any SpLD you may have. If a SpLD is found, the report will recommend what support would be useful to help with this. Do arrange to see your SpLD adviser when you have had all your assessments to ensure you know about and can access any support available to you.

## Be sure to access any help available

Your degree or Masters certificate won't say you are dyslexic or have another SpLD or if you accessed any available support. Many students get the assessment report and leave it at that. The extra support is there to help you **achieve your full potential**, so do access this.

Students who take up one-to-one study support and/or use assistive technology often comment that they don't know what they would have done without it.

Living and studying at university is very demanding and this extra stress can make dyslexia and other SpLDs more apparent. Many dyslexic/SpLD students manage well until crunch points such as their dissertation or exams. Make sure you know what is available and how to arrange support **before** you hit these moments, so you are prepared.

## One-to-one study skills support

Universities vary in how they provide one-to-one support. Some organise this for you and you attend sessions within the university; others may put you in touch with a tutor for you to arrange times and where to meet. Alternatively, you may have to contact an agency that arranges this for you. Refer to your assessment information to find this out.

# How to get the most out of one-to-one sessions

One-to-one support sessions for dyslexic/SpLD students at university cover many of the skills outlined in this book. The advantage for you is that these will be tailored to your particular requirements.

It will be useful for the tutor to see a copy of your diagnostic assessment report at your first meeting and they will be able to answer any questions you have about it. The tutor will of course discuss your strengths and limitations and suggest strategies to cope with these.

It is useful if you come prepared for sessions with any course information (or how to access these on the VLE). If you have any particular concerns you want addressed, do speak up! Sometimes it can be daunting speaking about your difficulties but your tutor is there to support you through it and it should be a positive experience.

If, for any reason you wish to change tutor, do contact your university's SpLD team. Don't worry about this, they are used to such requests. It is YOUR right to access the support, but it must work for both you and your specialist support tutor.

# References

Autistica (2014) *Autism*. Available at www.autistica.org.uk/autism/. Accessed 20 Jan 2017.

Batliwala P, Cattermole J, McLaren R and Simpson R (2016) 'Reading strategies and speed reading', in S Hargreaves and J Crabb (eds) *Study Skills for Students with Dyslexia* (3rd edn). London: Sage, pp. 84–6.

Brain.HE (2006) *Exams and Revision*. Available at www.brainhe.com/students/types/ExamsandRevision.html. Accessed 26 Feb 2017.

Buzan T (2003) *Use your Head*. London: BBC, p. 64.

Cottrell S (2008) *The Study Skills Handbook*, 3rd edn. Basingstoke: Palgrave Macmillan.

Diversity and Ability (DnA) *Resources*. Available at: www.dnamatters.co.uk/resources/. Accessed 10 Jan 2017.

Dyspraxia Foundation (2013) *What is the Overlap Between Dyspraxia and Dyslexia?* Available at: https://dyspraxiafoundation.org.uk/questions/overlap-dyspraxia-dyslexia/. Accessed 29 Feb 2017.

Genius Within (2013) *Neuro Diversity Venn Diagram* (based on a model by Mary Colley of DANDA (2006)). Available at: www.geniuswithin.co.uk/infographics-and-literature/neuro-diversity-venn-diagram/. Accessed 5 Feb 2017.

Kirby A (2013) *How to Succeed in College and University with Specific Learning Differences*. London: Souvenir Press.

Middlebrook RD (1990) *The Textmapping Project*. Available at: www.textmapping.org. Accessed 16 Oct 2011.

National Autistic Society (2016) *What is Autism?* Available at www.autism.org.uk/about/what-is. aspx. Accessed 14 Jan 2017.

Patrick A (2015) *The Dyspraxic Learner: Strategies for Success*. London: Jessica Kingsley.

Pauk W (2001) *How to Study in College*, 7th edn. San Francisco, CA: Houghton Mifflin.

Rose J (2009) *Identifying and Teaching Children and Young People with Dyslexia and Literacy Difficulties. An independent report from Sir Jim Rose to the Secretary of State for Children, Schools and Families*. Available at: www.education.gov.uk/publications/ eOrderingDownload/00659-2009DOM-EN.pdf. Accessed 7 Jan 2012.

Simpson R (2016) 'How to make the most of your lectures', in S Hargreaves and J Crabb (eds) *Study Skills for Students with Dyslexia* (3rd edn). London: Sage, p. 54.

Torgesen JK (1981) 'The study of short-term memory in learning disabled children: goals, methods and conclusions', in K Gadow and I Bialer (eds) *Advances in Learning and Behavioural Disabilities*, vol. 1 (pp. 117–50). Greenwich, CT: JAI Press.

Westminster School (n.d.) *The Forgetting Curve*. Available at: www.rgsinfo.net/subject/ learning%20support/pdfs/TheForgettingCurve(Westminster).pdf. Accessed 7 Jan 2012.

Williams K (1995) *Writing Essays*. Oxford: Oxford Centre for Staff Development.

Williams K and Carroll J (2009) *Referencing and Understanding Plagiarism*. Basingstoke: Palgrave Macmillan.

Williams K and Reid M (2011) *Time Management*. Basingstoke: Palgrave Macmillan.

# Useful contacts

## Getting support at HE

### Applying for DSA

DSA-QAG (Disabled Students Allowances Quality Assurance Group):
www.dsa-qag.org.uk

DfES (Department for Education): www.gov.uk/disabled-students-allowances-dsas

yourDSA: www.yourdsa.com

### Assessment

NNAC (National Network of Assessment Centres): www.nnac.org

PATOSS (Professional Association of Teachers of Students with Specific Learning Difficulties):
www.patoss-dyslexia.org

ADSHE (Association of Dyslexia Specialists in Higher Education): http://adshe.org.uk

# SpLD support

## Dyslexia

Being Dyslexic: www.beingdyslexic.co.uk

BDA (British Dyslexia Association): www.bdadyslexia.org.uk/educator/bda-services-educators

Dyslexia Action: www.dyslexiaaction.org.uk

DAN (Dyslexia Adult Network): http://dan-uk.co.uk

Dyslexia-SpLD Trust: www.thedyslexia-spldtrust.org.uk

Helen Arkell: www.helenarkell.org.uk

NNAC (National Network of Assessment Centres): www.nnac.org

The Codpast: http://thecodpast.org

## Dyspraxia

Dyspraxia Foundation: http://dyspraxiafoundation.org.uk

Movement Matters: www.movementmattersuk.org

## Autism spectrum disorders

National Autistic Society: www.autism.org.uk

## AD(H)D

ADHD Foundation: www.adhdfoundation.org.uk

ADDIS (National Attention Deficit Disorder Information and Support Service): www.addiss.co.uk

ADDers: www.adders.org

## Dyscalculia

BDA (British Dyslexia Association): www.bdadyslexia.org.uk/dyslexic/dyscalculia Dyscalculia Information Centre: www.dyscalculia.me.uk

# Useful resources

ADHD & You: www.adhdandyou.co.uk.

BrainHE: www.brainhe.com/index.html.

British Dyslexia Association *Policy, Research, Identification and Intervention for Maths Learning Difficulties and Dyscalculia*: www.bdadyslexia.org.uk/common/ckeditor/filemanager/userfiles/Dyscalculia_resources.pdf. Accessed 22 Jan 2017.

Diversity and Ability (DnA) *Resources*: www.dnamatters.co.uk/resources/.

Leicester University online study guides: www2.le.ac.uk/offices/ssds/accessability/study-skills/study-guides.

Sheffield University – Study skills for students with dyslexia: http://dyslexstudyskills.group.shef.ac.uk/.

Teaching for Neurodiversity: A Guide to Specific Learning Difficulties: http://dyspraxiafoundation.org.uk/wp-content/uploads/2016/09/P16-A_Guide_to_SpLD_copy_2.pdf. Accessed 22 Jan 2017.

The Codpast: http://thecodpast.org/ News and contemporary views

VARK: http://vark-learn.com/.

Wyvern Training Portal: Assistive Technology Training Videos: https://users.wyvernportal.co.uk/courses/main-videos.

# Index